All through the Day,
All through the Year

All through the Day, All through the Year

All through the Year

Family Prayers and Celebrations

David B. Batchelder

Augsburg Books
Bringing Families Together
for Children & Families

ALL THROUGH THE DAY, ALL THROUGH THE YEAR
Family Prayers and Celebrations

Acknowledgments
Scripture passages are from the New Revised Standard Version of the Bible, copyright © 1946, 1952, 1971, 1989 by the Division of Christian Education of the National Council of the Churches of Christ in the USA. Used by permission.

Page 17: "Lord, fill this night with your radiance. . . ." excerpt from the English translation of *Liturgy of the Hours* © 1974, International Committee on English in the Liturgy, Inc. Used by permission. All rights reserved.

Page 17: "Be our light in the darkness, O Lord, . . ." from *The Book of Common Prayer,* © 1979 of the Episcopal Church.

Page 44-45: "I was hungry: And you gave me food . . ." and "Lord Jesus Christ, may our Lenten fasting . . ." excerpts from *Catholic Household Blessings and Prayers,* © 1988 United States Catholic Conference, Inc., Washington, DC. Used with permission. All rights reserved.

I wish to thank Dainty Pastry Shoppe, 339 Depot Street, Latrobe, PA 15650 for generously sharing their recipe for pascha bread.

Cover and interior illustrations by Barbara Knutson
Book and cover design by Michelle L. Norstad

Library of Congress Cataloguing-in-Publication Data
Batchelder, David, 1951-
    All through the day, all through the year : family prayer and celebrations / David Batchelder.
    p. cm.
    ISBN 0-8066-4039-1 (alk. paper)
    1. Family—Religious life. 2. Family—Prayer-books and devotions—English. 3. Church year—Prayer-books and devotions—English. I. Title.

BV4526.2 B36 2000
249—dc21   00-026667

The paper used in this publication meets the minimum requirements of American National Standard for Information Sciences—Permanence of Paper for Printed Library Materials, ANSI Z329.48-1984. ♾ ™

Printed and bound in Hong Kong by C&C Offset Printing Co., Ltd

AF 9-4039

04   03   02   01   00   1   2   3   4   5   6   7   8   9   10

With gratitude to God for the nurture
I have received all through the years:
from my parents who have supported me,
my children—Mark, Heidi, Scott, and John—
who continue to teach me,
and my devoted wife, Nancy,
who has helped to make our home a place of worship.

Contents

Introduction

Of all the gifts parents can pass on to their children, faith is the most precious. While it is God alone who "gifts" us with the ability to believe, Christian parents can become God's partners in this enterprise. The promise of God, which is ours in baptism, calls us into a lifetime of growing up into Christ. In those Christian traditions in which the practice is for parents to present their children for baptism, the vows we parents take remind us of our faith-building partnership: we promise to live the Christian faith and to teach the faith to our children. The heart of our role as Christian parents is sharing and living out that faith with the children God gives us.

This book offers suggestions on how to structure faith building into the often chaotic but exciting life of Christian families. In doing so, it describes ways of being a Christian family in action as well as in word. Such ways give a shape and structure to our lives and draw us into the mystery and splendor of God's continuous self-giving. We deepen faith as we practice faith, and this book is about such practice—especially in our worship and praise of God. Thus this book offers practical suggestions for family worship in the home—and ways to discover joy and wonder in such worshiping. Both parents and children can come as learners to the experiences offered here, and if they do, parents will soon discover what a gift it is to learn the faith anew with their children—a gift they bring to us, a gift we should treasure.

What I remember most about family devotions when I was a child is the tension that arose because my parents tried to make our devotions "just like church"—namely, serious, somber, and correct. Fortunately, churches today are recovering a sense of worship as celebration and joy. If family worship borrows from church practices, we must include this sense of joy and celebration and not feel the need to do it "perfectly."

A family setting invites creativity and spontaneity—elements often (necessarily) lacking in the more formal setting of church. Therefore, the following pages do not offer detailed road maps but compass headings that plot directions for family worship. Feel free to pick and choose, borrow and adapt—to develop faith rituals that have special meaning for your family.

My wife and I had the chance to rethink our parenting strategies in midstream, so

to speak. Seven years after our daughter was born, we were surprised with another pregnancy. Our surprise grew to near shock when we discovered we would have twins. But we also discovered an unanticipated gift in this surprise: the opportunity to rethink ways we could live together as a Christian family. And this time around, we could involve our older children in the planning. This book shares some of our discoveries in family worship: rituals, symbols, and liturgies that have become important to us. These things have changed us by deepening our faith, knitting us more closely together, and—equally important—teaching us how to have fun worshiping together.

Five principles guide our family worship times. You will see these principles applied again and again in the suggestions that follow.

• Symbols are important; they evoke a sense of wonder, and they tap into the imagination.

• Too many words can drown family worship. Rituals can speak in place of words, and often young children can understand them more easily than words.

• Following the church calendar—the liturgical year of the church—helps us remember who we are as a family of faith.

• Bringing some language of church worship into our family worship helps link the two experiences closer together.

• Worship should include joy, and fun is an important element of joy. In every meaningful ritual of our family worship times, there is an element of "play."

The pages that follow offer ideas that weave our faith into the structure of our daily lives. As we pay attention to special times that touch our faith, we discover how to live our faith not only through our days but all through the year—and, ultimately, throughout our lives. Such a pattern of living and celebrating our faith can bring together the often discordant and disconnected fragments of our hectic lives. The thread tying our lives together as families will be this rhythm of worship and ritual, which gently shapes us with the joy of God's loving faithfulness.

A word or two about patience is in order here. Faith rituals in the home are like delicate gardens: we plant them little by little, year by year, and we tend them carefully as they become part of our family life. We may be disappointed if we attempt too much too soon. Another mistake can be to smother something new we are trying by overexplaining it. Understanding grows with experience: we learn as we do. With patience and persistence, we will see the flowers of faith bloom in our family's life, in our celebration of special events throughout the year, and in our relationships with one another. The process requires effort, but it promises a rich reward. In the end, we are shaping the faith of the next generation. God will take our best efforts and fill them with grace.

So turn the pages and sample the suggestions. Try the ideas on "for size." See how they fit your family's day, your family's year. Remember: these are only compass headings to help you chart a course. Use your imagination to shape and tailor what will work best in your family. Become a maker of faith rituals as you live and share your faith with your family.

All through the Day

Catching a Vision

I confess that we are a soccer family. Each autumn, our lives are filled with practice schedules and soccer games that stretch to the limit our capacity to juggle school-work, household chores, and music lessons—not to mention the basic and necessary task of feeding ourselves.

Such a pace has now become the norm for many families. Each additional child in a family compounds the complexity of fitting everything in. The family desperately needs a way to be centered as a family. Our common baptism and faith gives us this center, but we must find a way to tap into that together. Joining in prayer and praise at key moments in family life is an important way to counter the unhealthy effects of our hectic pace. Some excellent opportunities for family worship come at mealtimes and bedtime. Christians have long recognized these occasions as special moments for worship: they call us to thank God for the good gifts that sustain us and for gracious protection through the night.

In the suggestions below is an affirmation that we "taste and see that the Lord is good" as we share the gifts of food and drink at meals. At bedtime, we gather the joys and disappointments of our day and trustfully lay them in God's keeping, in order to receive again the gift of peaceful rest.

Mealtimes

In our family, the meal that most of us eat together is dinner, so dinner has become an important sharing time for us. We often begin the meal with a ritual that has a long tradition in the Christian church. A large white candle is placed in the middle of the table. After we're all seated, one child strikes a match and lights the candle. This act calls us to God's presence and reminds us that we are God's people. One member speaks a line based on Psalm 70, "O God, come to our assistance." The rest of us respond, "O Lord, hasten to help us." Next we sing a verse from a favorite hymn— usually chosen by one of the children.

Our meal prayer is introduced with words we use each week in church: one member says, "The Lord be with you"; the rest reply, "And also with you." The first speaker then says, "Let us give thanks to the Lord our God." We answer, "It is right to give God thanks and praise." By using this "church" language at our mealtime, we remember that what we do in one place is closely related to what we do in another.

In addition, our children are helped to learn this language by heart even before they are able to read it in a church bulletin. Finally, this ritual and these words imply that our family dinner table is very much like the table around which God's family gathers with the risen Christ to share bread and wine.

Following this dialogue, we sing or speak together one of the family prayers we have learned. Our repertoire of prayers numbers about a half dozen. Sometimes one of us offers a spontaneous prayer, but we have found that traditional, written prayers offer the greatest participation. By using them over and over, we commit them to memory for life. Such prayers also connect us to other Christians who pray or have prayed them.

Here are some of our regular prayers—beginning with our favorite:

Lord Jesus, be our holy guest,
our morning joy, our evening rest,
and with our daily bread impart,
your love and peace to every heart.

Welcome Jesus be our guest
to share our company,
and by your gifts may we be blessed
to serve you thankfully.

Lord, you clothe the lilies,
you feed the birds of the sky,
you lead the lambs to pasture,
the deer to the waterside,
you multiplied loaves and fishes,
and changed the water to wine;
come to our table as giver
and as our guest to dine.

Join us, Lord, at this meal
and gather us in love,
that food and drink and table talk,
will lift our hearts above.

Sometimes our prayers include the words of peace we exchange each Sunday in church. If there has been a squabble between siblings or some other tension-raising matter, one of us says, "The peace of Christ be with you all," and everyone else responds, "And also with you." This simple exchange is surprisingly effective at restoring family communion: it reminds us of the gift of peace that is ours, and it places all of us—together—within the circle of Christ's peace. (The section on Lent on page 42 explores in more detail this important aspect of family worship.)

Our family also follows the ancient tradition of concluding prayers with the words,

"Bless the Lord" and the joint response, "The Lord's name be praised."

The ritual of mealtime prayers has many attractive benefits and is adaptable to busy family life. Prayer rituals connect us to the church of the past and the church of the present—particularly the church we attend each week. Such prayer makes use of symbols and actions, songs and verses—all appealing and important aspects of faith nurture. The act of praying before meals also slows us down and enables us more fully to enjoy our food and our time together. Even the meal itself takes on an added dimension and significance when we begin or end it with prayer. Such a flexible pattern of prayer forms for daily use can be easily adapted to receive other elements during the festivals of the church year, such as Christmas or Easter. Finally, in the prayers we offer, we discover new things about one another and grow closer as a family united by faith.

Bedtimes

Bedtime is sometimes the most trying part of the day for families, especially when very young children are involved.

The resistance to going to bed is a natural part of childhood, but sometimes it comes from

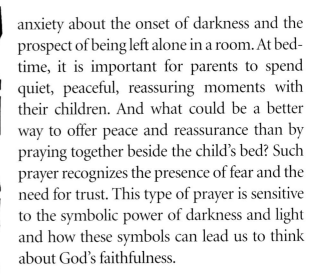

anxiety about the onset of darkness and the prospect of being left alone in a room. At bedtime, it is important for parents to spend quiet, peaceful, reassuring moments with their children. And what could be a better way to offer peace and reassurance than by praying together beside the child's bed? Such prayer recognizes the presence of fear and the need for trust. This type of prayer is sensitive to the symbolic power of darkness and light and how these symbols can lead us to think about God's faithfulness.

Differences in children's ages will usually mean different bedtimes for everybody, so it may be best to have bedtime prayers with each child as she or he goes to bed. This has been the pattern in our home. Prayer time with our twin sons waits until all bathroom duties have been completed and they are tucked in bed. We begin by singing the first verse of Mary's song, the "Magnificat." We chose this song for its attitude of joy and peace: it expresses Mary's hope and trust in God's promise. This song has long been prayed by the church at evening, when darkness settles over the land. Another fitting bedtime song is the "Nunc Dimittis," the words of trust and joy Simeon spoke when he was shown the infant Jesus—a fulfillment of God's promise that Simeon would see the Savior of the world.

There are many wonderful songs and hymns a family could choose for bedtime prayers: "All Praise to Thee, My God This Night;" "Now the Day Is Over;" and "Abide with Me, Fast Falls the Eventide" are just some of these. Check your church hymnal—or ask your pastor or church musician—for words and music to the songs of Mary and Simeon, as well as other choices for bedtime songs.

Following the song, we say a prayer together that is appropriate for the end of the day and the onset of sleep. This, too, has remained unchanged since we first began. We pray:

> *Lord, fill this night*
> *with your radiance.*
> *May we sleep in peace*
> *and rise in joy,*
> *to welcome the light*
> *of a new day in your name.*
> *We ask this through Christ our Lord.*

One thing remains in our bedtime ritual: before we leave the room, with moistened thumb we make the sign of the cross on each child's forehead, speaking their name with the words, "Remember your baptism and be thankful. You belong to God."

These words recall for us all the power and significance of our Christian identity. With this identity comes God's faithful promise and presence from which nothing can separate us—not darkness, not sleep, not fear, nor even death itself.

Bedtime prayer works deep in a child's consciousness and has the power to build a habit of trust that can last a lifetime. Here are several other suitable bedtime prayers that easily can be memorized through repetition and prayed by parent and child together:

> *Be our light in the darkness, O Lord,*
> *and in your great mercy*
> *defend us from all perils and dangers*
> *of this night;*
> *for the love of your only Son,*
> *our Savior Jesus Christ.*

> *We bless you, God,*
> *for the day just spent,*
> *for laughter, tears,*
> *and all you've sent.*
> *Grant us, Good Shepherd,*
> *through this night,*
> *a peaceful sleep 'til morning light.*

Send angels, Lord, around us here,
to keep our dreaming free from fear.
When morning comes
to bring the day,
show us how to follow your way.

In darkness, Jesus, come be near,
to give us peace 'til light appears.

Jesus, Shepherd, stay this night
bring us safe to morning light.

Family Activities

Faith building is not limited to mealtimes and bedtimes. Any traditions that provide times of joy and sharing can open families to the presence of God in ordinary things of daily living. What is needed are imaginative ways to help family members see life as a "God with us" communion. The following ideas are intended to spark your imagination and help you dream up activities that let your family discover God's abiding presence alive and active in, with, and through each of them.

Game Time

Technology has multiplied the number of amusement choices for families. In most homes, we can find a television in nearly every room, two or three VCRs, computer games, and electronic handheld games. All these items keep our children riveted to video screens and, often, isolated from other human communication. As entertaining as they may be, these gadgets do not provide the kind of social interaction offered by old-fashioned board games or card games or dominoes. Even though some board games can now be played on the computer, there is no substitute for gathering the family around a table for lively competition with Monopoly or rummy or dominoes. Family game times can build lasting memories.

When I was a child, my family loved playing games together—and they still do to this day. Those family game times drew us into many contests, often revealing much about who we were and what was important to us. Winning and losing within a family is part of the character building that helps us into maturity. Family games can play an important role in teaching us to have fun without being obsessed with winning.

Now that I am a parent, I am introducing my own children to the pleasure of board games as alternatives to computers and video entertainment. Though we do not play together as often as my childhood family did, our game time around the table is always met with enthusiasm.

Our current favorite is a game of dominoes called "Mexican Train," and we top off the evening by breaking out the lemonade and popcorn. The game allows us to express our unique personalities as we experience laughter, frustration, surprise, and joy. Above all, game time offers a shared space in time to bond with one another—to "become" as a family.

Try game time in your own family. Carve out an hour or two on a Friday or Saturday night, and invite your children to choose a favorite game or learn a new game together. An alternative to playing games is working a jigsaw puzzle. Remember to spice up the time with special treats.

Flashlight Hikes

With a creative twist, plus a touch of serendipity, even the most ordinary activities become ways for families to discover new things in themselves and God's world. For example, how about taking a flashlight hike with your family? An hour or so before bedtime is an excellent time for such a hike—especially if it comes as a

surprise. Equip everyone with a flashlight and take a walk around your neighborhood. It's a cozy feeling to walk in the dark with just a beam of light to see the way. This can be fun on a summer night or even in the middle of winter. Try a flashlight hike during a heavy snowfall, making fresh tracks in the snow and watching the flashlight beams bounce off the thick flakes. Upon your return, mix up a cup of hot cocoa to take the chill out of the bones.

For years, I have taken my children on a winter walk through snow to "see Jesus." Not far from our home is a solitary statue of Jesus—all that remains of an old Catholic girl's school that burned down many years ago. After donning scarves, hats, boots, and mittens, we trek out through the accumulating snow, pretending we're crossing a glacier on Mount Everest.

Picnics and Snacks in the Great Outdoors

Children will delight in almost any activity if snacks and drinks are involved. Whether it's a visit to a local arts and crafts fair or just a walk into the park for a little Frisbee, your family outing will take on a special "treat" quality if you pack snacks and tasty drinks. Grab a school backpack and gather whatever the children might enjoy as their snack. Make sure there is plenty to drink on a hot day. Invite your family to view their time in God's creation (and the snack!) as a blessing by reciting this verse from Psalm 118 as you begin your outing: "This is the day that the Lord has made; let us rejoice and be glad in it." Outdoor adventures begun with a blessing and topped off with favorite snacks will add richness to childhood family memories.

Dancing in the Living Room

I am a baby boomer, and when it comes to pop music, I love the "oldies" (even though my taste tends toward classical). Fortunately for me, the golden oldies have made a revival through television commercials and movies. As a result, my kids are just as fond of "Duke of Earl" and "Barbara Ann" as I am.

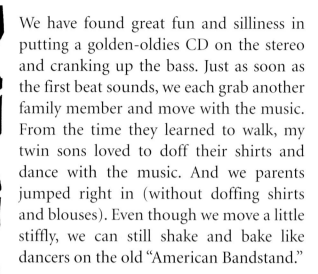

We have found great fun and silliness in putting a golden-oldies CD on the stereo and cranking up the bass. Just as soon as the first beat sounds, we each grab another family member and move with the music. From the time they learned to walk, my twin sons loved to doff their shirts and dance with the music. And we parents jumped right in (without doffing shirts and blouses). Even though we move a little stiffly, we can still shake and bake like dancers on the old "American Bandstand."

This is family silly time—a time of laughter, a time to eschew all self-consciousness. It is also a time of shared vulnerability. Were a stranger to look through the window, I might feel stupid; but with my family . . . well, it's just old dad pretending and being silly. Such nights with the golden oldies are great equalizers—we all get silly together—and great sources for everybody's family memory book. To this day, when I hear certain songs on the radio, they bring me a smile and a chuckle because I can visualize us all in our living room together.

Cleanup–Giveaway Day

Organizing family-room bookcases and cleaning up toy shelves are probably the last things anyone in our family wants to do, but they are necessary. Cleanup time is easier if everyone shares in it. And it can be fun—even meaningful—if there's a bigger purpose to the shared activity. Closets packed with outgrown clothes, shelves overflowing with old games, crates stuffed with abandoned cars and action figures—all these may be potential sources of pleasure for someone else. When we sort through belongings with the intention of giving things away, we learn about stewardship, and we help others derive joy from things that gave pleasure to us.

Choose a time when everyone can help sort through old toys and clothes. Don't rush through the task; take your time. Encourage children to imagine and talk about who might become the new owner of each plaything or clothing item. Then be sure to bring your children along to the thrift shop so they can see how their belongings change hands. Or let them wrap the items and deliver the gifts to community shelters or charity groups. Help your children find joy in seeing others enjoy possessions that once brought pleasure to them.

Reading and Telling Stories

Stories and bedtime are as natural and pleasurable a combination as milk and cookies. When the lights are dim and your children are tucked in for the night, read them a story. Or make one up and tell it to them. Stories that appeal to the imagination are especially good; they feed our minds on possibilities of what might be, what could be. The imagination is a gift from God that needs constant nurture. Purchase read-aloud books and collections of stories, or find ones in the library. (Be sure the stories for bedtime are full of pleasant and hopeful images!) Practice reading with inflection and expression so the characters and story come to life. Or consider telling an original story. My boys have always loved hearing adventure stories in which they are the heroes who miraculously rescue other family members in peril.

All through
the Year

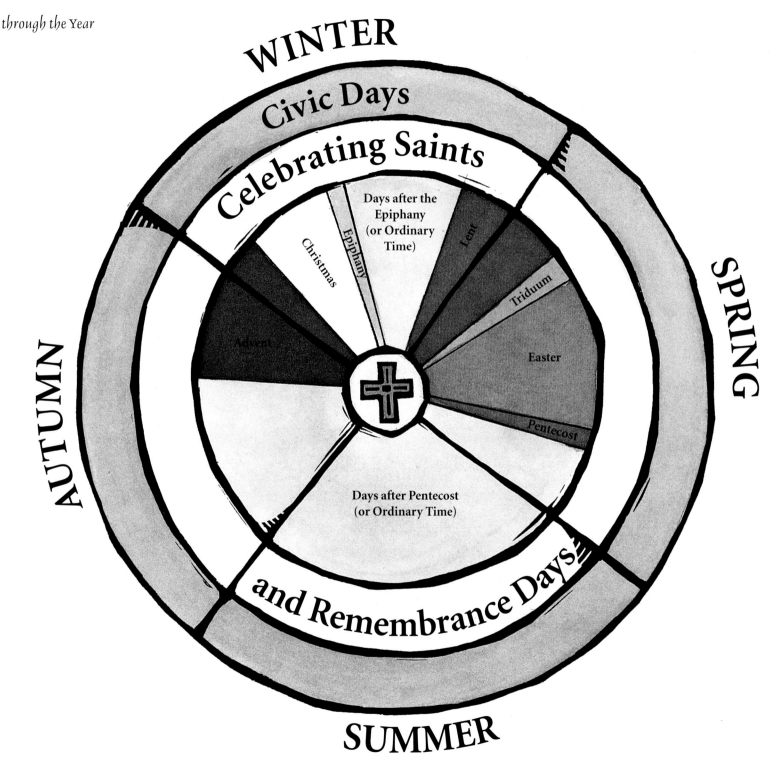

Catching a Vision

In our kitchen hang two calendars: the school calendar with all the school year's important events and a large, decorative, month-at-a-glance calendar with ample space under each day to note all family appointments and events. Should either of these calendars be misplaced, our family would be thrown into chaos. These calendars reflect our lives and give them shape. They tell us what we are about as a family and what events-in-time have importance for us.

The church, too, has a calendar that tells what events-in-time are significant for God's family. Since ancient days, this calendar has formed and informed the lives of Christians, helping them not only recall and observe key events in salvation history, but also participate in the very meaning of Jesus' life, death, and resurrection for the world. Just as my home calendars help me shape the days and months of my family's life, so the church's liturgical calendar helps shape our lives as God's blessed people.

The Church Year

Toward the end of every autumn, around the time we gather for Thanksgiving Day, the church begins another new year. This unusual reckoning of time points to our identity as members of the faith community, an identity given to us because God has chosen to act graciously in time on our behalf. Remembering God's deeds has given shape to the way the church keeps time because, in this way, we experience afresh the power of God's new life in our present moment. Thus, the Church Year offers us a wonderful pattern for living, learning, and celebrating our faith through the way it opens us up to rhythms of festivity that fit as comfortably in the home as they do in our churches.

The heart of the Church Year lies in its two great festivals: Christmas and Easter. Christmas always falls on December 25, while the time for Easter is based on the lunar calendar but always falls on a Sunday. Each festival is preceded by a period of preparation. Patiently attending to God's Promises in Advent, we arrive at Christmas and Epiphany, a twelve-day celebration of God's coming in Jesus. Counseled and guided to readiness in Lent, we arrive at Easter and Pentecost, a fifty-day celebration of Jesus' dying, rising, and presence among us.

As the Christmas festival bids us marvel at God's coming in human flesh and the glory revealed in "God-with-us," so the Easter festival bids us marvel at Jesus' willingness to die a criminal's death for the sin of the world, his burial, and his astonishing vindication the third day as God raised Jesus from the tomb. Thereafter, Easter celebrates the continuing presence of this same Jesus, who leads us in service to others, promises to be with us always, and, with God, sends us the power of the Holy Spirit on the Day of Pentecost. In the church's time between these two great festivals, we are encouraged to live faithful lives. Through a rich diversity of scriptures, we are drawn into the stories of Jesus as well as women and men who struggled to live in faith. This pattern of the church—keeping time as ordered to faith—is meant to give us a deep remembered sense of whose we are, God's presence in the world, and our gracious future. As we ourselves participate in this manner of keeping time, we experience the wonderful power of God's love to freshly shape our living each day.

This book offers a pattern whereby families can bring the joy of the Church Year into their daily lives in ways that allow everyone to be drawn together in the grace of God. Often families will find that experience in church can be imported to the home so that the relationship between home and church is strengthened. In this way, home and church share the blessing of a common faithfulness.

Remembrance Days

Also included on pages of the church-year calendar are boxes noting special remembrance days for each month of the calendar year. The boxed dates are included to alert your family to the possibility of additional celebrations remembering people and events important to the Christian church.

Following the church-year section in this book is a more detailed description of each remembrance day, along with celebration ideas—ways you might invite the presence and memory of each person or event into your family.

Advent

Advent begins the church year by calling us to wait for Christ's coming. This season has its earliest roots in Spain and Gaul (France), where it was first celebrated. The word *Advent,* which comes from Latin, means "to come;" and the weeks of Advent spark a sense of eagerness and anticipation. After all, when we are expecting the arrival of someone or something important, we organize our lives around this anticipated event. Advent begins on the fourth Sunday before Christmas Day, December 25. Each Sunday leading up to December 25 is counted as the first, second, third, and fourth "Sunday of Advent."

A season of waiting seems almost out of place in today's world of instant gratification: our culture is used to having what it wants and having it now. We don't like to wait for anything. Thus, we should not be surprised that our society has little appreciation for Advent.

Yet we Christians know that God's promises often take time to be born. Our spiritual ancestors waited thousands of years for the fulfillment of God's Word. Countless generations of Hebrews hoped they would see the promise come true in their lifetime; and as they faded into history, each generation handed on that promise to the next generation. Finally, in the fullness of time—when God saw that all was ready—a young woman named Mary bore the final months of waiting as the promised Savior grew within her.

Advent traditions are oriented toward the theme of waiting in hope. They are designed to help us abide patiently, faithfully, and confidently. During this season, we learn that waiting and believing are nurtured by prayer. Advent brings together all three—waiting, believing, and praying—in a season that prepares us for the promise of God's coming at Christmas.

Advent Wreath

In the long and bitter winters of ancient times, people in northern Europe found comfort and hope in branches of trees that never lost their green. When formed into a circle (perhaps around a wagon wheel) and given the light of candles, this winter greenery became early Advent wreaths, reminders of the birth of Light at Christmas. Immigrant German Lutherans brought this custom of the Advent wreath to North America, where it continues to speak the deep meaning of God's promised light in a season and a world of darkness.

The Advent wreath can form a focal point for family worship, especially if the wreath is set in the center of the dinner table. (Ours rests in a jungle of salad dressings and salt and pepper shakers.) The lighting of the wreath at each evening meal can lead into a prayer or meditation that reflects the meaning of Advent. If this causes children to wait a little longer before digging in to the meal, they get a small taste of what Advent is about.

Though Advent wreaths are available commercially, I prefer the home-built variety. Our wreath is a scrap of plywood, about a foot square, spray-painted green. We glued four plastic pipe fittings onto the corners as candle holders, and hammered metal staples partway into the wood so that plastic (or real) greenery could be inserted. Four purple or royal blue candles go into the holders, and a larger, free-standing white candle is placed the middle. We dress up the wreath with pine cones and artificial red berries. It's not elaborate, but it

looks surprisingly good and serves our needs nicely.

More important than how the Advent wreath looks is that it be used. The first candle is lit on the first Sunday of Advent, and on every day of that week. On the second Sunday, a second candle is lit along with the first. These are lit each day of the second week. A third candle is lit on the third Sunday; and so on through all four weeks of the season. This growing light in the midst of winter darkness is a sign of God's promised light of Christmas.

The privilege of lighting the candles can be shared among family members. In our family, we substitute the Advent wreath for our mealtime prayer candle so that Advent devotions can be incorporated into mealtime prayer easily.

When the wreath is first lit each year, a blessing such as this might be said by all:

> *Faithful God, who sent us Jesus,*
> *make this wreath smile with joy*
> *and these candles burn brightly*
> *with the truth of your Word.*
> *Through Jesus Christ our Lord.*

Advent Calendar

Originating in Germany, the custom of Advent calendars quickly spread to other countries. It's a delightful way to harness the energy of eager children whose anticipation of Christmas grows with each passing day. Advent calendars are well suited to family worship around the Advent wreath—either at mealtime or at night before bed. Traditionally, one window or door is opened each day until Christmas, revealing an illustration and a scripture reference related to Advent and Christmas. Families can read these Bible verses and discuss the illustrations for brief Advent meditations. Many bookshops and Christian supply stores sell Advent calendars at modest prices so that a new one can be used each year.

Some families might choose to create their own calendars, with each member contributing original artwork (Christmas symbols, seasonal images, Bible story illustrations) on small, same-sized squares. Affix these picture squares to a large sheet of posterboard, and cover each with a slightly larger square of blue or purple construction paper that can be opened as a "door" or "window." Number each door, for the days of Advent, and on its reverse side, write a Bible verse or hymn name. As the family opens each door to reveal the artwork and Bible verse, the artist can talk about what the picture means and then read the scripture verse or hymn.

Home Decorating

Our society puts Christmas decorations out as early as possible—earlier each year, it seems—thereby overlooking Advent waiting. But we do not have to follow this example. There is virtue and value in accepting the discipline of waiting as a gift.

The discipline of Advent waiting can be captured in Christmas decorating when we carry out the decorating in steps. Rather than putting up everything in a mad frenzy when you finally find time to do it, designate specific days for progressive stages of decoration, so your home reflects the coming of Christmas rather than just its arrival.

For example, you might set aside a day for starting a Christmas-card display (that can be added to as more cards come in); another day can be designated for trimming the mantel; one day each week can be used for assembling and then adding to the crèche (more on this later); and one day can be spent putting up and decorating the tree. Families also might choose to decorate the house in stages—first the front

door and entranceway, next the hallway, then the family room, and so on—climaxing with the trimming of the tree. By extending this preparation time, you will discover a sense of growing anticipation as well as a more meaningful progression through Advent into Christmas.

In our home, the first stage of decorating commences on the first Sunday of Advent as we light electric candles in all the windows. For the first two weeks of Advent we light these only on Sundays. Thereafter, they are lit each evening as darkness settles.

Fireplace Mantel

The fireplace mantel presents a prime opportunity for one clear stage in decorating. If you don't have a fireplace mantel, a bookcase or the top of a piano will also work. In our family room is a brick mantel, which we keep bare until the second Sunday in Advent. On the eve of this day, candles, greenery, a red bow, and beloved nutcrackers appear. Our children look forward to this transformation in the family room because it signals that we have journeyed nearly halfway through Advent. As our home begins Advent in relative bareness and waits to be filled with Christmas blessings, we are reminded of our own lives before God.

Crèche

The crèche is a favorite decoration that is often assembled far too early. It can capture the beauty of Advent waiting and anticipation when it, too, is assembled in stages.

Begin by setting out an empty manger and a few animals—and the stable or shed, if this is part of your crèche. Shepherds and sheep might be placed nearby, ready to be moved from the "neighboring hillsides" when the time comes. Because the holy family should arrive at the stable on Christmas Eve, figures of Mary and Joseph might begin a four-week journey through the house as children move them, week by week, along the path from Nazareth to Bethlehem. The wise men, of course, must wait until Epiphany (January 6) before they arrive—long after shepherds have returned home praising God.

Our children have a wonderful time inventing new and unusual routes through the house for Mary and Joseph to reach the manger. Each year I am amazed by how the children remember—and look forward—to putting Jesus in the manger on Christmas Eve. When the crèche is incorporated into family worship, it is transformed from a mere decoration into a symbol that engages us and makes our Christmas richer.

When the creche is first arranged in its place for Advent, a prayer might be spoken or prayed in unison, such as the following:

Faithful God, who blesses us
in our waiting,
bless, too, this crèche,
which awaits your Son.
As the holy family journeys
to this manger,
prepare our hearts
to welcome his presence.
Through Jesus Christ our Lord.

Christmas Cards — We Receive

As we receive Christmas cards, we display them in various locations throughout the house. Last year, we hung them along the top of the wall near the ceiling. Some years we incorporate them into our mealtime prayer ritual, reading the verses and sharing news of the persons who sent them before adding the cards to a collection on the mantelpiece.

It is increasingly common for people to send family photographs in cards or as the card itself. We have a special place where all Christmas photographs are displayed. For our family, this becomes a wall of remembrance and thanksgiving. As each photo falls out of a newly opened Christmas card, someone tapes it to the paneled wall of our family room—near the telephone, where it is sure to be looked at again and again throughout the holidays.

Families also might consider offering a special evening or mealtime prayer for those friends and family members whose cards are received each day. Following the meal, children could display the cards in their customary place.

Christmas Cards — We Send

For many good reasons, families have trimmed the list of gifts they send to persons beyond the immediate family. One way to continue affirming your appreciation for those people no longer on the gift list is to send them homemade Christmas cards. One year, our family constructed Christmas card "masterpieces," which we sent to loved ones across the country. These "masterpieces" consisted of pieces of scraps that were made into colorful pieces of art. They have since become holiday decorations in the homes of our extended family as well as yearly reminders of the bonds of love and faith that tie us together.

Designate one night in December as a no-television evening of creative endeavor and family fun. Parents and children can gather materials for the card making: scraps of fabric, construction paper, remnants of ribbon, crayons, scissors, markers, and photographs.

If you have a growing family, it is meaningful to send a photograph along with your Christmas card. Such a picture may be found among vacation photos or, even better, you might have it taken for just this purpose. Invite all family members to help plan the picture: Will it be indoors or outdoors, at the home or in the park, along a trail, soccer field, or on bikes? What might family members wear or hold to express something about themselves, their interests, and personalities? This kind of planning gives the family a chance to think of and express itself as a unit as well as a collection of unique individuals. And a carefully planned, creative family photo makes a wonderful gift to loved ones and relatives.

Composing a family Christmas letter on the computer gives each family member a chance to exercise his or her independence and creativity. Everyone can take turns at the word processor, sharing a few experiences from the past year and special hopes for the future. Artistic family members might embellish the master copy with leaves of holly or a few bells before it is sent through the copier.

It might even be possible for several family members to compose a seasonal poem while others provide illustrations. The results could be printed in multiple copies and sent as the family Christmas greeting for the year.

Some people's cards deserve a special handwritten greeting appended to the printed letter or poem. Each family member can take a handful of such cards and write a note for the whole family. This gives everyone a special responsibility and asks him or her to think in terms of "us."

In all this activity, if a little break is called for you need only serve up a few holiday treats—cookies or candy and hot cocoa—to rejuvenate the troops.

December Remembrance Days

Dec. 1   Rosa Parks
Dec. 5   Wolfgang Amadeus Mozart
Dec. 7   St. Ambrose
Dec. 13   St. Lucia
Dec. 17   Dorothy Sayers

St. Nicholas Day

Within the season of Advent falls a special date that should not go unobserved. December 6 is St. Nicholas Day, the day when Bishop Nicholas died and was born into God's eternal kingdom. The real-life inspiration for the mythical figure of Santa Claus was a fourth-century bishop with a special concern for children and poor people. His fabled acts of kindness can inspire greater faithfulness and present an opportunity for selfless generosity in Advent. Observing St. Nicholas Day also can help restore the worthwhile origins of our culture's Santa Claus (who has now become almost a symbol for greed and commercialism) as well as providing a foretaste of the Christmas feast to come.

For nearly ten years, our family has celebrated the Feast of St. Nicholas. The night before this feast, my wife and I decorate the dining room with candles, hints of Christmas, and the makings of a breakfast feast. We awaken early on the morning of December 6. The table is set with our finest dishes, silverware, teacups, special pastries, and cinnamon rolls. In the center of the table stands a wooden figure of the kindly bishop (we found it in a Christmas store).

The purpose of this feast is to remember and celebrate St. Nicholas's example of compassion. Before we begin to eat, each family member draws another member's name from a hat. On St. Nicholas Day, we perform secret acts of kindness for the person whose name we have drawn. In this way we seek to be like Bishop Nicholas, who gave generously and secretly. At the end of our meal, we share this prayer:

God of joy and cheer,
we thank you for your servant,
the good bishop Nicholas.
In loving the poor,
he showed us your kindness;
in caring for children,
he revealed your love.
Make us thoughtful
without need of reward
so that we, too, may be good
followers of Jesus.

In many places on St. Nicholas Eve, it is traditional for children to put a pair of shoes outside their bedroom doors as they go to bed. In the morning, the shoes are filled with treats. Oranges are traditional delights for this occasion: they recall the legend of how Bishop Nicholas secretly gave a poor father three bags of gold for his three daughters—providing them a marriage dowry so they could avoid the fate of slavery.

Christmas

The season of Christmas lasts for twelve days, from Christmas Day (really beginning with Christmas Eve celebrations) until January 6, the Feast of Epiphany or Twelfth Night. The Twelve Days of Christmas are a period of celebration that date back to ancient times.

After keeping Advent, families are well prepared for twelve long days of celebration. Though children may at first feel cheated by having to wait for Christmas festivities, there is a terrific payoff when families claim all twelve days of the Christmas season.

Christmas Eve

Because I am a minister, our home must pay close attention to time on Christmas

Eve. Late in the afternoon (we calculate time backwards from when we must be at church), our family gathers around the kitchen table to begin our Christmas Eve ritual. Everyone has already showered and dressed for the evening. Because they have so much to look forward to on this night, we never have a problem motivating our children to be ready on time. What follows are traditions we share each year. These are easily adapted to a later time of the night.

Sleigh Bells and the Christ Candle

On Christmas Eve, it's time to embellish family worship with new sounds and rituals. The four Advent candles have been burning for a month, waiting to be joined by the light of the Christ candle. Tonight that new flame will be added!

Before lighting any candle, we shake a set of sleigh bells so their sound echoes throughout the house. The bells have not been heard since last December 24, but it is time to announce the transition from Advent to Christmas. (In our home, the bell ringing is a high honor that must be shared among our children from year to year.) Next, light all the candles—the Christ candle last.

"Noel! Christ is born for us!" speaks a child.

"Noel! O come, let us adore him!" reply the rest of us.

Then sing one verse of a favorite Christmas carol; choose one everybody knows by heart. During their early years, the twins could join in only on the chorus, but it was not long before they knew the verses, too—and this was well before they could read.

Blessing of the Christmas Tree

In our household, we decorate the tree the Saturday before the fourth Sunday of Advent; but wait to turn on the lights until we have shared the blessing of the tree on Christmas Eve. Blessings recognize that God created the world and all its creatures and that God's world is good. Such blessings also resolve to see God revealed in the ordinary gifts given each day.

Now is the moment to gather around the Christmas tree. There are two privileged roles in our family's Christmas Eve worship: the first is throwing the switch (or plugging in the cord) to light the tree; the second is offering a tree blessing such as the following:

> *God of our first parents,*
> *you gave Adam and Eve a taste*
> *of paradise*

amidst a garden of beautiful trees.
As we light this tree after weeks
of waiting,
stir in us the hope
of your blessed future,
where happiness and joy
are your eternal gifts.
All glory and honor belong
to you alone.

Placing Jesus in the Crèche

It is time to place the baby Jesus in the manger. For this occasion, it would be good for a child to read—or have read to him or her—the Christmas story from the Gospel of Luke (2:1-7), using a favorite version of the Bible or a children's Bible. When the figure of the baby Jesus is placed in the manger, a prayer, such as the following, might be prayed in unison:

> *Marvelous God who fills this night*
> *with wonder,*
> *we have arrived to welcome*
> *Jesus' birth.*
> *With cattle and shepherds we honor*
> *your gift.*
> *May his presence warm our hearts*
> *with tenderness enough*
> *for everyone we meet.*
> *And keep us always in your joy.*

Christmas Eve Meal Blessing

The bells have been rung, the candles are lit, the tree is glowing with light, and Jesus is snug in his manger. Now we sit down to eat.

Our Christmas Eve ritual requires that we move from room to room, processing from the table through the house, and back to the table again. This is not an evening to fuss over an elaborate dinner or one that will suffer from waiting for the ritual's completion. When we are seated for the Christmas Eve meal, one or all of us offer a prayer suited to the occasion.

> *Jesus our Savior,*
> *you are welcome here.*
> *With animals and angels*
> *we sing your praise.*
> *Fill us with joy*
> *for your gifts of love,*
> *given to all who hunger and thirst*
> *for your salvation.*
> *Warm our table with your presence*
> *that this meal may be a taste*
> *of all good things to come.*
> *Through Jesus Christ,*
> *the light of the world.*

Friends of Christ (Comites Christi) — Spreading Out Gift Giving and Receiving

The Christmas season has a series of built-in celebrations: the festivals of Comites Christi or "Friends of Christ." The first is St. Stephen's Day, on December 26; the second is St. John's Day on December 27; and the third is Holy Innocents Day on December 28.

Young children often reach a saturation level after opening five or six Christmas gifts. Why not save some gifts for these festivals? Reserve a few gifts for opening during the "Friends of Christ" festivals by marking them with phrases such as, "Open on St. Stephen's Day" or "Save for St. John's Day." Remember to set aside some of the adults' gifts, too, for these celebrations are not just for children. You will be surprised at how this turns Christmas into a season rather than a single day. On these days of Comites Christi, family worship can reflect the special meaning assigned to each. Here are a few suggestions:

The Feast of St. Stephen

St. Stephen's Day honors those who are poor, as did St. Stephen, one of the first deacons in the church, and good King

Wenceslaus. Wenceslaus was a prince of Bohemia who had great compassion for the poor people in his land. Legend tells us that during the harsh winters, the king secretly carried wood he had illegally cut from the forest and gave it to widows and orphans. Because he disguised himself, the king was once mistaken for a thief and beaten. In this way, King Wenceslaus followed the example of St. Stephen, who lived selflessly for others.

To celebrate this day, families might sing J. M. Neale's carol, "Good King Wenceslaus" at their evening meal or devotion. And this is surely a day when the life and story of Stephen should be remembered, perhaps with a reading from Acts 6 and 7. The following prayer might be used to conclude the reading and singing:

Lord Jesus, for our sake you
became poor and lowly.
We thank you for your servant
Saint Stephen and his kindness
for the poor.
Give help to all in need, especially
(name people and places known to
need help).
May we be like Stephen by caring
for the hungry and homeless
whom you have given
as our neighbors,
and make our table always a place of
welcome for the needy.
Through Jesus Christ our Lord.

Families might also celebrate by taking on special projects to help the poor and homeless—such as setting aside money at every meal to donate for the hungry, volunteering at the local food pantry or homeless shelter, or collecting and donating food items to a food bank.

St. John's Day

St. John's Day remembers the commandment found in John's Gospel (15:12-14) to love others as Christ loves us. An ancient story claims that John was given poisoned wine to drink, but he did not die. This story has led to the tradition of celebrating St. John's Day with new wine and using it in a special toast. Family worship could include the blessing of new wine and the sharing of a common cup. (Grocery stores provide nonalcoholic wine, which can serve as a merry beverage for this occasion.)

This day is best celebrated by acts of love and thoughtfulness in which family members extend kindness and service to neighbors. St. John's command about love might

be carried out by taking someone home-made bread, a fresh-baked pie, or a pot of soup; by shoveling your neighbors' drive-way; or by sharing a good book with peo-ple who are unable to leave their homes.

On this feast day a family prayer might be the following:

> *God of faithful love,*
> *we remember the commandment*
> *you gave through Jesus' faithful*
> *friend John.*
> *Teach us how to love*
> *by putting the interests of others*
> *before our own.*
> *As we share this meal,*
> *sweeten our hearts*
> *with the wine of gratitude*
> *for all your blessings.*
> *Through Jesus Christ our Lord.*

Holy Innocents Day

Holy Innocents Day commemorates the flight of the holy family to Egypt and King Herod's massacre of children in Bethlehem. The church has always looked upon these children as the first martyrs of the church, and their plight reminds us of innocent per-sons who suffer around the world.

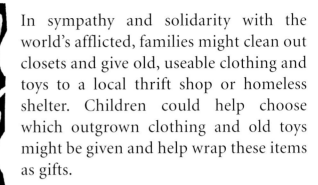

In sympathy and solidarity with the world's afflicted, families might clean out closets and give old, useable clothing and toys to a local thrift shop or homeless shelter. Children could help choose which outgrown clothing and old toys might be given and help wrap these items as gifts.

Or perhaps you could take toys or games to children confined to a hospital and stay to visit and play some of the games with them.

Evening prayer on this day could include all those who suffer—in your church or community or world. Before praying, you might discuss current news stories about disasters, famines, or war, helping one another focus concern on people around the world who need God's mercy. Family worship might include reading about the flight to Egypt and the slaughter of the innocents (Matthew 2:13-23). Here is a prayer suited to the special nature of this day:

> *God of the suffering,*
> *we know you feel pain*
> *for in Jesus you suffered with us.*
> *Heal the wounded,*
> *mend the broken,*

*and free all from forces bent
on harm.
Especially help the children
of the world
who depend on the mercy of others.
As the child Jesus was once driven
from his home in search of safety,
let this home and this table always
be a haven for those who hurt.
Through Jesus Christ our Lord.*

January Remembrance Days

Jan 1   Holy Name of Jesus
Jan 18   Confession of St. Peter
Jan 25   Conversion of St. Paul

Epiphany

Originating in the Eastern church, Epiphany celebrates the manifestation, "showing forth," of God's salvation to the Gentiles. In the Gospel of Matthew, we learn that early visitors to the Christ child were magi, who probably traveled from Persia (contemporary Iran) to visit Jesus sometime after his first birthday. Later in history, the tradition of the traveling kings merged with the Western celebration of Christmas based on Luke's narrative. Thus,

the Twelve Days of Christmas emerged as the season of the Nativity, beginning with Christmas Eve and Jesus' birth, and ending with Epiphany—the showing of God's glory to the world. As Jesus is the "light to the Gentiles," so Epiphany is a celebration rich in symbolism that includes light, incense, and gift giving.

Celebrated on January 6, Epiphany invites families to participate in rich, imaginative, and playful rituals. With a little planning, you can incorporate a number of delightful traditions into your family celebrations.

$20 + C + M + B + 00$ *(current year)*

In some European homes, it is customary at Epiphany to mark the lintel above doorways with symbols of blessing. Invite your children to mark your own front door with these symbols: the date, the initials of traditional names for the three Magi—Casper, Melchior, and Balthasar, and four crosses. Order these symbols in the following way, $20 + C + M + B + 00$ *(current year)*, with the four crosses representing the four seasons. In the new year, this marking serves as a blessing over the entire household. Be artistic and creative. The marking may be made with chalk or on a piece of cardboard that has been decorated with colored markers and designs.

A Meal Fit for Royalty

Epiphany is an ideal occasion for an extravagant feast. It is not necessary to toil all day preparing a complex meal. Serving family favorites—especially those of the children—will make the point that this meal is special. (It is good to remember that a child's idea of a feast may be quite different from that of an adult!) Special dishes, cloth napkins, and purple and gold crepe-paper decorations (colors of royalty, for the three kings) will add to the mood.

And what is a feast without candles—especially ones that celebrate a festival of light amidst darkness? Candles should be used as the only light source in the room. Use every candle holder you can find to bathe the dining room in light. The act of lighting them alone will instill a sense of wonder and awe for this night.

Three Kings Cake

As a special dessert for this meal, bake a spice cake into which three small nuts or dry beans are inserted before baking. (You can also insert the nuts into the cake after it is baked and then ice it over before eating.) Tradition says that whoever discovers a nut or bean in his or her piece of cake is chosen as a king or queen for the evening. (Families with fewer or more than three children may want to adapt this tradition so no one feels left out. In our family, we've often had four magi!)

Costumes

Costumes can add an especially festive touch to this evening's ritual. Children (and adults too!) can transform themselves into royalty simply by donning bathrobes and fancy scarves, and you can create your own crowns using cardboard, colored paper, and markers, perhaps gluing on sequins and glitter. An old Halloween costume might provide a beard or two for the kings. These royal garments should be worn throughout the evening celebration. Make sure to take a photograph of your family royalty to remember the occasion.

Blessing the Home

There is a rich tradition of house blessing at Epiphany, for the festival coincides with the arrival of a new year. This blessing can beautifully supplement the "20+C+M+B+00" markers over the doorposts.

For our ritual, we cut a small evergreen branch from a bush or tree in our back garden and use it to sprinkle "water of blessing," evoking our identity as those God has welcomed in baptism. Evergreens symbolize the power of eternal life because they never lose their green, even in the dead of winter. Singing a hymn such as "We Three Kings," our family journeys through the house, sprinkling water in each room. Each of our children gets to sprinkle his or her own room. No one is left out. Even the family dog follows obediently in this procession.

Bringing the Magi to the Crèche

During the course of the evening's procession, the family can complete the journey of the magi figurines from their last resting place to the manger where the baby Jesus is waiting. This could be done while singing "We Three Kings." (By this time, the kings have sat atop every bookcase and cabinet in our house, and their arrival at the final destination has been eagerly awaited.) Once the magi are in place, read the story of their visit in Matthew 2:1-12.

Incense

As a reminder of the sweet-smelling gifts the magi offered Jesus, families might scent their home with incense. Different varieties of incense can be purchased at specialty shops and used for this celebration. (Sticks of cinnamon boiled in water or baked in an oven also can add a wonderful

spicy scent to the air.) Some incense can be lit directly while some needs to be sprinkled over a piece of charcoal that has been lit in advance. The incense smoke wafting toward the ceiling is a wonderful symbol of our prayer rising to heaven. Our sense of smell is powerful and lasting, and the aroma of incense will call forth memories of Epiphany in our children's minds for years to come.

Words Suited to the Feast

As with each of the other seasons and feast days, the words we use deepen the meaning of what we celebrate. With the lighting of the candles, these words of blessing might be spoken:

> *God of wondrous light,*
> *by a star you led the wise men*
> *to your newborn son.*
> *Give us your light so that we can see*
> *to follow where you lead*
> *and live always in the joy*
> *of your abundant blessing.*
> *Through Jesus Christ, the light*
> *of the world.*

Here is a prayer that might be used after reading the story of the magi and placing them in the crèche:

God of love,
you sent your son
to his home with us.
As the magi welcomed Jesus
with gifts on bended knee
so we welcome you
into heart and home.
Bless each room
with your presence and peace
that we may be filled
with your Spirit of joy.
In your holy name we pray.

Save a Gift for Epiphany

Every family member should reserve one last gift to open on the night of Epiphany. If there are several games or puzzles among the gifts, the gift opening can lead to an evening of joyful family interaction.

February Remembrance Days	
Feb. 2	Presentation of Jesus
Feb. 14	St. Valentine
Feb. 18	Martin Luther

Lent

The forty-day season of Lent derives its name from the Latin word for "lengthen." During Lent, the days grow longer as the world prepares to reawaken into spring. Begun in the darkness and death of winter, Lent recalls the forty days and forty nights Noah and his family spent on the ark, the forty years of Israel's wandering in the wilderness, and the forty days of prayer and fasting that Jesus spent in the desert. Focused on the Easter promise of new life and renewed faith, Lent invites Christians to look honestly at themselves as they seek to be strengthened in the call to be Christ's disciples. Traditionally Lent is when the church prepares candidates for baptism at Easter. Also, Lent is a time for almsgiving (sharing what we have), prayer (for ourselves and others), and fasting (special resolve to work on greater faithfulness).

The character of Lent as a time of renewed commitment and service suggests many possibilities for families. Because Lent itself is a kind of spiritual journey, any one or two of the following suggestions can provide a rich spiritual experience for families embarking on their own Lenten pilgrimage.

A Return to Discipline

Lent is a wonderful time for families to recommit themselves to a practice of prayer at dinnertime and at bedtime. If busy schedules or neglect have eroded family prayer time, Lent offers the opportunity to rebuild these practices that give us life and keep us centered in God's love. As the father welcomed home his prodigal son, so Lent is our welcome to return to those spiritual practices that give us life and keep us centered in God's love.

Rituals That Heal

Every family needs to keep a watchful eye on its interpersonal relationships so that feelings of anger, resentment, or bitterness aren't allowed to grow. Often the pace of life prevents us from dealing with the baggage we build up over time. Our well-being is best served when we face the hurt we have caused and grant each other forgiveness. This kind of healing can take place through rituals of reconciliation. Such rituals are especially well suited to Lent, the season of penitence and spiritual preparation.

My family has sometimes gathered for the evening meal in icy silence or heated debate over some unresolved injustice or lack of kindness. By incorporating a ritual of reconciliation into our mealtime prayer, we manage to find again the peace our common baptism in Christ gives us. Soon after, our table is buzzing with good humor and discussion of the day's activities, and a sense of community is restored.

Here are a few possibilities for building rituals of reconciliation into your own family:

Psalm 51—Evening prayer around the table might include a scripture reading such as Psalm 51 ("Create in me a clean heart, O God, and put a new and right spirit within me"). Prayer and family conversation could then focus on those things that wound the heart and those that heal.

Common Confession—Your family might offer a prayer of confession in unison, perhaps one used in church the previous Sunday. Once the ice is broken and the words are spoken, the hurt can be released. Below is another prayer that could be said together. It might be typed out so all can pray aloud together. One person could speak a line at a time with others repeating; or, if used often enough, the prayer could be learned by heart.

God of love,
you are generous in grace
and we stingy of heart.
Forgive the hurt
we have brought others
so that we all can be free
from anger and live together
in the peace of Christ.

Sharing the Peace of Christ—This ritual is appropriate following a family prayer of confession, such as the one just described. It invites family members to express the transforming power of God's forgiving grace. Sharing the peace of Christ can also be done apart from prayers of confession. Many times these words and gestures have cut through hard feelings and returned our family members to a mutual affection. The language offered here comes from the liturgy for Sunday worship.

One person—perhaps a parent—speaks the words in light print, and everyone responds with the words in bold:

> *Because God has forgiven us in*
> *Christ, let us forgive one another.*
> *The peace of Christ be with you all.*
> ***And also with you.***

Following these words, each person clasps the hand of every other family member, saying, "Peace be with you."

Praying and Acting for the Poor and Hungry

Though this is important all year round, especially during Lent we are reminded to carry the suffering of others in our prayer. Such prayer shapes the minds and hearts of the very young to keep a concern for all those who suffer or are in need.

In our home, each night in Lent a different family member leads the prayer below: The rest of us respond with the text in bold type.

> *I was hungry:*
> ***And you gave me food.***
> *I was thirsty:*
> ***And you gave me drink.***
> *I was a stranger:*
> ***And you welcomed me.***
> *I was naked:*
> ***And you clothed me.***
> *I was ill:*
> ***And you comforted me.***
> *I was in jail:*
> ***And you came to see me.***

Lord Jesus Christ,
may our Lenten fasting
turn us toward all our brothers
and sisters
who are in need.
Bless this table, our good food,
and ourselves.
Send us through Lent
with good cheer,
and bring us to the fullness
of your Passover.
In the name of the Father,
and of the Son,
and of the Holy Spirit.

Offering for the Poor

Collecting money or food for the poor is an act of discipleship that recalls the practice of almsgiving. Many church denominations emphasize such giving through special seasonal offerings. All denominations also have hunger funds, and some offer structured disciplines of giving. Worldwide organizations and denominational initiatives that respond to disasters provide additional ways for families to express their Lenten devotion.

On a smaller, more personal level, your family might assemble "health kits" of toothpaste, soap, and other toiletries, or collections of canned goods to donate to homeless shelters or food pantries in your community. These are wonderfully concrete ways for children to identify with the brokenhearted whom God is near. Contact your church or other local agencies about these or other ideas.

March Remembrance Days	
Mar. 10	Harriet Tubman
Mar. 17	St. Patrick of Ireland
Mar. 25	The Annunciation to Mary

Centering on the Cross

The central symbol of the Christian faith is the cross. This is an especially appropriate image for a Lenten journey with Jesus to his crucifixion. As Advent family worship is enriched by the symbol of the Advent wreath, so Lenten worship is well-served by the symbol of the cross.

Families might choose to make or purchase a simple cross to hang in the area where they eat and have devotions. The cross can serve as a focal point for Lenten prayer that recalls the way of the cross.

Our family hangs a crucifix in our kitchen area to aid our reflection of Christ's suffering

and death. On Easter, this cross is replaced with a bare wooden cross to mark our passage from Lent into Easter. Lent offers families the opportunity to appropriate faith rituals from the diversity of Christian traditions even if some of these rituals were not part of the families' background. We remember our call to follow Jesus by remembering to whom we belong.

Making the sign of the cross can be especially appropriate during Lent, when we remember our baptism and the mark of Christ through which we become Christians. By tracing the sign of the cross on our foreheads at the conclusion of each Lenten prayer, we remember our call to follow Jesus, and we remember the price that he paid to make us his own.

Making Ashes from Palms

Many families save their palms from Passion Palm Sunday services. These can be used for a special ritual on the Ash Wednesday that begins next year's Lent. Ashes are a biblical sign of sorrow and repentance, and they have a deep significance for Lent, symbolizing our mortality and utter dependence on God. If your church has no Ash Wednesday service or does not use ashes, consider imposing ashes on one another at home. In a metal bowl, burn the palms you

have saved. After they have cooled, grind them into powder and add a few drops of olive oil to mix them into a paste. Now you can use them for your family ritual.

Family members can serve one another, each marking a small cross on the forehead of a parent, brother, or sister. As you mark the forehead with ashes, say to one another, "From dust you came and to dust you shall return." Such words remind us that our lives on earth are only temporary, and we depend in faith upon God's promise to bring us to eternal life. It is never too early to begin this ritual with children to shape their understanding of our constant need for God. It is a lesson learned over and over again throughout a lifetime.

Memorizing Scripture and Hymns

Lent invites us to consider how we are feeding our spiritual lives with the good things of God. In past generations, congregations strongly encouraged children and adults to memorize scripture passages. Unfortunately, this is no longer true of many churches. There is much value to be gained by memorizing particular scripture passages.

One of the great gifts we can give our children is the ability to recall God's scriptural promises during personal crises and at times of joy, loss, doubt, or loneliness. Consider, for example, the reassurance offered in these words from the Twenty-third Psalm: "Even though I walk through the darkest valley, I fear no evil; for you are with me."

With regular guidance and encouragement from their parents, children can commit such wonderful words and promises to memory. Here are suggestions for a few significant scripture passages that children and adults might learn:

Genesis 12:2-3, Psalm 23, Psalm 121, Proverbs 3:5-6, Isaiah 40:30-31, Isaiah 41:10, Matthew 6:33, Matthew 11:28-29, Luke 4:18-19, John 3:16, John 11:25-26, John 13:34-35, John 15:9-10, John 17:20-21, Acts 10:43, Romans 8:37-38, Romans 12:1-2, Ephesians 2:8-10, Philippians 1:6, Philippians 4:6-7, Colossians 3:1-3, Hebrews 11:1-2, Hebrews 12:1-3.

Perhaps families could learn these passages by reciting them together—one passage each day for a week—as part of their meal-time prayer. Or family members could take turns sharing with the rest of the family the verse they are memorizing, reciting it and talking about what it means to them.

Imaginative Forms of Fasting

Up until recent times, Christians of many traditions observed personal fasts during Lent—giving up specific foods, habits, or pastimes. At its best, such "fasting" helped people remember the sacrifice of Jesus and recall their own need for God. At its worst, fasting became a kind of legalistic, and often thoughtless, Lenten "obligation."

When undertaken with careful thought and imagination, Lenten fasting can help Christian families focus on their shared spiritual life. You may decide it is appropriate to bring some eating habits or uses of time under special discipline—giving up meat, dairy products, candy, or soda; not watching television or movies; or giving up playing video games—in order to focus more fully on the sacrifice of Jesus and on our call to serve one another.

When undertaking a fast, it is good to consider that some traditions break the fast after sundown each day, or if not each day, certainly on the Lord's Day, which is reckoned as beginning at sundown Saturday.

It is not necessary always to think of a fast as giving something up. Instead, you might consider adding something to your Lenten observance. Such a "fast" might include the

writing of affirming notes to family and friends, visiting sick people in the hospital, preparing a meal each week for elderly persons in the church, or offering to baby-sit for a single parent who may need an evening away from children. Such possibilities are limited only by our imagination.

> **April Remembrance Days**
>
> April 4   Martin Luther King Jr.
> April 9   Dietrich Bonhoeffer

Triduum: Maundy Thursday, Good Friday, Holy Saturday

Baptism signifies our incorporation into Christ's victory over the powers of sin and darkness. According to Scripture, by water and the Spirit of God in baptism, our sinful natures are buried with Christ in his death and we are raised to new and eternal life with his resurrection.

The "mystery" of Christ's triumph over sin stretches across the three days of Jesus'

arrest, crucifixion, and resurrection. Beginning on sundown of Maundy Thursday (with Jesus' Last Supper and his arrest), continuing on Good Friday (with his death by crucifixion), extending through Holy Saturday (with his burial), and concluding at sundown on Easter Sunday (with his rising from the grave and appearances to his followers), these are the three most amazing days in the church's calendar. Calculated according to the Jewish reckoning of day and night (from sundown to sundown), this period of time is known as Triduum (from the Latin meaning "three days"). The events of these days form one continuous drama that offers us a marvelous opportunity to return to the heart of baptismal faith. Here are a few possibilities for home celebration:

Music and Silence
The music with which we fill our homes can influence our sense of where we are in the church's time. The season of Lent, and especially Maundy Thursday, Good Friday, and Holy Saturday, is well suited to listening to the Passion oratorios and requiems of Bach, Beethoven, Hayden, Faure, and Rutter, or such hymns as "When I Survey the Wondrous Cross," "Beneath the Cross of Jesus," "Amazing Grace," and "Were You There?"

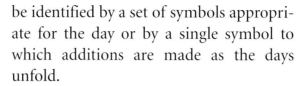

Purposely choosing our selection of music to reinforce the mood of the church season can heighten the spiritual meaning of these holy days. Even refraining from music altogether is an appropriate form of abstention that prepares a family for Easter rejoicing.

Regulating Pace

By choosing to slow down and back off activities during this weekend, families recognize the importance of this time and remind one another of their shared identity as baptized followers of Christ.

Preparations for this slow-down might mean doing the food shopping, laundry, cleaning, and other errands earlier in the week. Families might take time at the table on Monday to list all the chores and duties that need to be done and then assign jobs to everyone. Thus, the preparation for Triduum becomes a team effort shared by all.

Creating Symbols and Rituals That Mark the Days

Symbols are important because they engage more than one of our senses and are capable of speaking what cannot be said in words. Each day of Triduum could be identified by a set of symbols appropriate for the day or by a single symbol to which additions are made as the days unfold.

Passion Stones

Almost twenty years ago, I found two milk-colored stones with cavities and shapes that reminded me of human skulls. These stones became our family's "passion stones." On Maundy Thursday we set the stones out in our living room, one leaning upon the other to form a kind of "tomb." They remain in this position until after the Easter Vigil late on Holy Saturday, when they are separated (the "tomb" is opened). Our children are given turns to handle the stones. They are symbols that enrich our family worship during Triduum.

Triduum Cross

One year, each family in my congregation made a purple felt cross and five smaller felt symbols that could be attached to the cross (using small pieces of hook-and-loop tape) as the family progressed from Palm Sunday to Easter Sunday. The symbols were a green palm branch for Jesus' entry into Jerusalem; a loaf and chalice for Maundy Thursday; a cross for Good Friday; a tomb closed with a stone for Holy Saturday; and a butterfly (added to the center of the

cross) for Easter morning. This Triduum cross became part of each family's prayer ritual at dinner on these nights. For each day, one of the following prayers and Bible readings was used.

For Palm/Passion Sunday

Faithful God,
in Jesus you visited the holy city.
Many cheered while others prepared
for your death.
The enthusiasm of your friends
could not quiet their fear.
We know their weakness because we,
too, are often afraid.
Draw us near you in faith and trust
so that we can be strong followers of
Christ our Lord.

Scripture readings: Matthew 21:1-11, Mark 11:1-10, or Luke 19:29-40

For Maundy Thursday

Servant God,
in Jesus you showed us how to serve
one another.
Teach us this love,
which sets us free from worrying
only about ourselves,
so that we can care
for those around us.
And give us the grace

to forgive others as you have
forgiven us
though Jesus Christ, the servant
of all.

Scripture reading: John 13:1-17, 34-35

For Good Friday

Suffering God,
in Jesus you yourself
have tasted death.
We grieve for this broken world
and long for its healing.
Embrace us all—
those who follow you,
those who ignore you,
and those who oppose you—
with grace that is stronger
than death itself,
and bless us with your salvation.
Through Jesus Christ our Savior.

Scripture readings: Matthew 27:32-44, Mark 15:25-41, or Luke 23:26-43

For Holy Saturday

Patient God,
in Jesus you carried the sorrows
of this world.
Comfort those who mourn and lift
the burden of our pain.
Fill your people with faith in your

*power over sin and death
so that we may live in the joy
of your redeeming love.
Through Jesus Christ our Lord.*

Scripture readings: Matthew 27:57-61, Mark 15:42-47, Luke 23:50-56, or John 19:38-42

For Easter Sunday and Easter Season
*Wondrous God,
in Jesus you confused the soldiers,
confounded your disciples,
and broke the power of death.
With joy we worship you for your
victory over evil
and ask that you keep us forever
in the safety of your love.
Through Jesus Christ,
the Risen Lord.*

Scripture readings: Matthew 28:1-10, Mark 16:1-8, Luke 24:1-12, or John 20:1-18

Shaping the Family Schedule around Corporate Worship

For much of the year, families shift and adjust their schedules around school, scouts, instruments, and sports. While these experiences and activities can help build skills and confidence in our children, they also help to fragment family life.

Holy Week and Triduum ask families to organize their schedules around the worship life of their congregation and the church year. These experiences and activities build spiritual skills and confidence and help to bring families together. By altering family mealtimes, cutting short baseball practice, and postponing piano lessons in order to participate in the rich worship life of the church, families remind one another of their special identity as God's family. To make such schedule alterations is itself an act of worship. (Participating in church worship should not be seen as a substitute for worship in the home; rather it is complementary.)

Easter

Since ancient times, Easter has been regarded as the jewel in the crown of the church's year. Not only does Easter predate Christmas as a time of celebration, in the early centuries of the church, Easter also embraced the meaning of Christ's incarnation and birth. Only in later centuries did Christmas and Epiphany emerge as separate festivals.

Easter has never been identified with a fixed date on the calendar. Instead, it is always celebrated on the first Sunday after

the first full moon following the spring equinox. Although this method of setting the date can be confusing, it is rich in symbolism. In the Northern Hemisphere, Easter falls after the annual triumph of light over darkness—when the hours of daylight once again exceed the hours of darkness. Thus, nature itself bears witness to what God has done in Christ.

The heart of Easter is the wonderful drama of Jesus' death, resurrection, and ascension—followed by the coming of God's Holy Spirit and the birth of the church. As with Christmas, Easter day begins the celebration rather than ends it. Based on the chronology of Luke and Acts, the fifty days of Easter include forty days from Jesus' resurrection until his ascension into heaven (at that time, Jesus told his followers to wait for power from on high) and the ten days in which his followers awaited the promised power (Acts 1:8).

Pascha Bread for Easter Dinner

Many traditions celebrate Easter by eating special foods that are made from eggs, butter, cream, and cheese—products that had been given up as part of the Lenten fast. Pascha bread is a favorite holiday treat made rich with dairy products and egg yolks. This bread often can be purchased from local bakeries, or it can be baked at home using the recipe below. If you bake it at home, consider making it a special Easter project involving the children. Let them decorate the bread with a bit of frosting and colored sprinkles, perhaps in the form of a cross.

Our family orders two such loaves each Easter and shares them at our Easter dinner with a glass of wine or grape juice (unfermented wine) using the traditional Jewish blessing. First a glass of wine or grape juice is shared by all and someone speaks, "Blessed are you, O Lord, our God, ruler of the universe, for you give us the fruit of the vine." Then, as the bread is broken and passed around the table, one person speaks, "Blessed are you, O Lord, our God, ruler of the universe, for you bring forth bread from the earth." This tradition has the effect of associating a special thanksgiving ritual with the blessing of the Easter meal.

Here is the recipe for pascha bread from a favorite bakery of mine:

Pascha Bread Recipe
¼ cup water
3 tbsp. granulated sugar
1 tsp. salt
1 tbsp. milk powder
2 tbsp. regular shortening
2 tbsp. of Hi-Ratio shortening
      (emulsified or cake shortening)

1 large egg
2-½ cups bread flour
¾ ounces compressed yeast
1 cup raisins (optional)

Directions:

Combine all ingredients in a large bowl. Because this is a rich bread, you will need to mix it at medium speed for 20-25 minutes (mix until dough becomes smooth and pliable). If raisins are used, add them to the dough for the last minute of mixing. Finished dough should have good elasticity.

Round the loaf and place it into a greased 8" cake pan. Cover and allow it to rise in a warm place until doubled in size. Place into a 365° oven for 40-50 minutes or until done. (The slightly lower temperature allows the rich dough to bake throughout.) When cool, add icing and decorations, if desired.

Easter Egg Hunts

The tradition of eggs at Easter reaches back to the earliest centuries of the Christian church, and the game of hiding eggs was probably a gift from German immigrants who brought the fable of the Easter Bunny to this country. This custom is one example of the joyful play that often attends festival seasons.

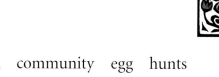

Unfortunately, community egg hunts almost always take place before Easter—usually on Holy Saturday—when our Triduum observance requires quiet preparation for the Easter Vigil. Frustrated by this fact, I decided many years ago to organize a family egg hunt on the afternoon of Easter Sunday. In order that my children wouldn't feel cheated by not participating in the community egg hunt, I went all out in my plans. Over the years our family egg hunts have included treasure maps, riddles, Bible clues, homemade videos, tape recordings or codes to be deciphered, photographs with clues, and even an auction. The result has been eager excitement in my children, a continual challenge to top the last year's effort, and a growing reputation for elaborate egg hunts. Even my college-age son and high-school daughter look forward to this annual event.

This family tradition helps us enter into the joy of Easter with a spirit of playfulness and sharing that affirms life. The fun and delight seems all the more appropriate after celebrating Easter with our local church. I am convinced that our family Easter egg hunts will survive the passage of several generations.

Keeping Triduum Symbols in Place

One significant way to communicate to our children that Easter is a season—not just a day—is to keep Triduum symbols in place for the fifty days. It is also helpful to continue using the Easter mealtime prayer throughout the season.

Easter Decorations

In our culture, much is made of the Easter Bunny and the season has a definite feel of commercialism and consumerism. To counteract this trend, try recovering colors and symbols that speak of God's Easter promise: life conquering death. Decorate cardboard or construction paper crosses with colored tissue paper or foil, giving them a stained-glass appearance. Cut butterfly shapes from cardboard, and decorate these with paints, markers, or colored paper before hanging them in windows or from the ceiling. Spend a Saturday morning coloring eggs, and then decorate these with Easter words and symbols.

May Remembrance Days	
May 8	Julian of Norwich
May 27	John Calvin
May 31	The Visitation of Mary to Elizabeth

In the paragraphs below are additional ideas for the fifty days of Easter.

Good Shepherd Sunday (4th Sunday of Easter)

One Sunday during the Easter season is known as Good Shepherd Sunday. Its name and emphasis come from the Gospel story in John 10, where Jesus calls himself a good shepherd who knows and loves and lays down his life for his sheep.

The beautiful image of Jesus as a good shepherd tending his sheep and lambs offers a wonderful way to help young children grow in their awareness of God's love and care. Also, this Sunday always includes the reading of Psalm 23, one of the best-loved passages from the Bible.

Parents can help their children reflect on these beautiful words and images and reinforce what the family has heard in church. One way to do this is by making "family sheep" to hang around the kitchen. Let children cut out sheep from poster board (one for every person in the family), glue on cotton ball "wool," and write a family member's name on each sheep. Someone might also make a shepherd's staff to hang from the light fixture over the table. Be sure to read

Psalm 23, perhaps in unison. Over time, this psalm could be committed to memory as part of the treasure of scriptures.

On this day, it is also appropriate to offer a mealtime prayer that uses the image of Jesus as the Good Shepherd.

> *We bless you, Risen Lord,*
> *as the Good Shepherd who gave*
> *himself for us.*
> *May we feast upon your love*
> *and kindness*
> *as we share this meal*
> *which you have given.*
> *Continue to guide us*
> *with your rod and staff,*
> *so we will follow in the path*
> *you lead.*
> *Through Jesus, the Good Shepherd.*

Pentecost

Pentecost owes its origins to an ancient agricultural festival of Israel in which first fruits of the barley harvest were offered to God. Added to this background is the Jewish Festival of Booths, which recalls God's faithfulness as the Hebrews journeyed through the wilderness from Egypt to the promised land. Each year during this festival, the Jews make booths or temporary shelters in which to live for a week in order to remember their heritage.

The outpouring of God's spirit took place during a celebration of this feast, enlarging its meaning for Christians. Luke describes the events of Pentecost in Acts 2:1-21. One hundred and twenty disciples were gathered to pray and wait for the promised Spirit, as Jesus had instructed them. Suddenly, the sound of a mighty wind filled the room, and tongues of fire appeared over the heads of the disciples, and all of them began praising God in different languages!

Pentecost is a day to be marked by fire, the color red, festivity, and surprises, and a warm welcome extended to all.

You Cannot Have Too Much Red!

Pentecost demands we pull out all the stops and go crazy with red: red crepe paper, red balloons, red tablecloth, red napkins, red juice as a beverage, red Jell-O, a bowl full of strawberries—perhaps even a shrimp appetizer with red cocktail sauce. And naturally, of course, each family member should wear some item of red clothing. Do not underestimate the impact such preparations can make on children: this is a special—red-letter—day!

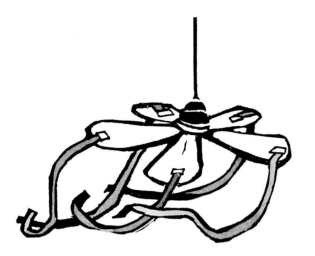

Fire at the Table

Lots of red candles add to the visual imagery of a domestic Pentecost celebration. Several years ago, I picked up at a flea market a black wrought iron candelabra that holds seven candles. Each year this fifty-cent bargain is the flaming centerpiece of our Pentecost table.

Feasting and Festivity

Pentecost is a day of joyful feasting, a celebration of God's graciousness. Let your mind run with how this might shape your family's menu and events for the day. Perhaps you will barbecue special foods over the grill or pack a picnic of favorite outdoor foods. How about family games of croquet, badminton, kickball, hide-and-seek, or volleyball? Do not treat this Sunday as just another day.

Wind Socks

Try hanging strips of red, orange, and yellow ribbon or crepe paper from the blades of ceiling fans (turned on low) for a visual reminder of the "wind" of the Spirit.

Gifts-of-the-Spirit Mobile

A favorite decoration for our family Pentecost is a mobile of red cardboard cut-out flames suspended from twisted coat hanger wire. On each flame is written one of the gifts of the Spirit mentioned in Isaiah 11. This is hung near the screen door where the breeze keeps it in constant motion. Something as simple as this helps children associate the meaning of Pentecost with the Holy Spirit and the Spirit's presence in the home.

Hospitality

As Pentecost proclaims God's welcome for people of every race and nation into one community, so a family's Pentecost celebration might involve hospitality to others—friends, family, even new persons in the church or neighborhood. What a powerful witness this offers for what God has done to heal divisions and make us one in the Spirit.

A Pentecost Prayer

God of wind and fire,
send your Spirit upon us.
Make our hearts burn with love
for all your children.
Rekindle our gratitude for this feast
and for every good gift,
so that we always have a spirit
of generosity
towards everyone we meet.
Fill our lives with joy and our faith
with courage.
Through Jesus, who with you
sent us the promised Comforter.

June Remembrance Days

June 14	Basil the Great
June 22	Thomas More
June 24	Birth of John the Baptist

July Remembrance Days

July 11	St. Benedict of Nursia
July 24	Thomas á Kempis
July 28	Johann Sebastian Bach

August Remembrance Days

Aug. 6	Victims of the atomic bombings
Aug. 13	Florence Nightingale
Aug. 28	Augustine of Hippo
Aug. 31	John Bunyan

September Remembrance Days

Sept. 5	Mother Teresa
Sept. 13	John Chrysostom
Sept. 18	Louis Pasteur

October Remembrance Days

Oct. 4	Francis of Assisi
Oct. 17	Ignatius of Antioch
Oct. 31	Reformation Day

Observing the Remembrance Days

One of the great truths of our faith is that the Christian church is one body in Christ that even death cannot divide. This understanding undergirds the church's affirmation of "communion of saints" in the Apostles' and Nicene Creeds. The church's presence and witness to the faithfulness of God is a blessing in each generation, so that we can affirm with the hymn "For All the Saints":

O blest communion,
fellowship divine!
We feebly struggle,
they in glory shine;
Yet all are one in Thee,
for all are Thine.
Alleluia! Alleluia!

It has always been a great source of encouragement for Christians to remember those who preceded us in faith and to consider their example (see Hebrews 13:17). Tradition has shaped this remembering in the form of a calendar of the saints. Though the concept of sainthood was a source of disagreement at the time of the Reformation, many Protestant churches today are adopting calendars of remembrance days—not only to remember spiritual leaders whose faithfulness gave birth to their denominations, but also to recall the powerful influence of saints of old.

What is suggested in this book is a modest calendar to honor some saints, Christian and civic leaders, and special events that can be meaningful for families with children. Included are hints as to how you might invite the presence or memory of each person or event into your family for the day. Remembrance days for saints of old always fall on their "death day," as this is the day on which they are born into eternal life. We have included other days to recall some significant events from the New Testament, church history, or national history that should be remembered with gratitude. These dates could be written on the family calendar most often consulted or you might prefer to make and decorate a separate family calendar of the saints. Perhaps this calendar also could carry names and dates of "family saints"—ancestors, relatives, and friends whose faithful witness should be remembered.

How your family chooses to treat each day is up to you. Perhaps you might include a mention of it in thanksgiving during mealtime or bedtime prayers; to this end you will find some prayers included here. It may be that some days will lend themselves to particular creative expressions of remembrance. Even if no special attention is given to some of these days, their presence on the family calendar will spark awareness and might elicit a question or two from a child. This subtle consciousness raising is an important influence in building a sense of the "communion of saints."

Once again, the list is only suggestive and should be amended to suit each individual family. Remember to surround your family with a company of saints as diverse and inclusive as is God's family. This means making sure there are persons of different ages; both men and women; persons of all races and nationalities; those whose witness is in ministries of justice, peace, evangelism, and healing; and, finally, persons from every age of the church. Such diversity will enrich your family's sense of what it means to be part of the whole people of God from every time and place.

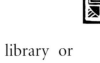

November ✠

1—All Saints' Day

All Saints' Day (All Hallows' Day) is a feast day in the church that remembers and celebrates those who have died in the faith. Their faithful witness—in life and in death—encourages us in our struggle to remain faithful to our God.

Consider attending your church's worship service for this day, or attend the service of another church. Give thanks for the saints of your congregation who have died in the last twelve months. Think about your own family and those members, both living and dead, who have been strongly dedicated to living their faith. Their witness is part of your family's heritage.

20—Leo Tolstoy (1828–1910)

Tolstoy was one of the greatest Russian writers. In his books, he wrestled with questions of morality and Christian ethics. One of his most beloved short stories is called "Where Love Is, There God Is Also."

This story has been retold in many versions and is available as a videocassette called *Martin the Cobbler*. Check a library or video rental store for the film; then set aside time to view and discuss it on this day.

22—C.S. Lewis (1989–1963)

Clive Staples Lewis was a British scholar, an Oxford professor, and the author of many books. Of particular note is his series The Chronicles of Narnia, a children's classic of seven volumes that uses fantasy to teach children about faith and God.

If you do not own these books, purchase them for your family or check them out of the library. Then read them together. Adults enjoy them as much as children!

December ✠

1—Rosa Parks (1955)

On this day in 1955, an African-American woman refused to give up her seat on a bus in Alabama. She was protesting unfair laws that said black people had to sit in the back of public buses. For this "crime," Rosa Parks was arrested by the police. However, her example inspired many people, who boycotted the buses for a year. Rosa Parks's courage and sense of justice contributed much to civil rights reform.

Go to the library or search the Internet for articles and biographical information about this remarkable woman. Give thanks to God for people who show the courage of their convictions in confronting injustices.

5—Wolfgang Amadeus Mozart (1556–1791)

Mozart, an Austrian composer, is one of the world's greatest musicians. His love of life and gift for music have given the world great joy. Let this day be filled with such joy by sharing the gift of Mozart's music.

One of Mozart's most famous compositions is his "Eine Kleine Nachtmusik," or "A Little Night Music." A recording of this piece would make fine dinner music.

7—St. Ambrose (340–397)

A bishop and pastor, Ambrose was greatly influential in Western Christianity. His writings are an invaluable source of insight into the life and faith of the early church. As bishop, Ambrose baptized St. Augustine and served as his teacher.

Each of us is blessed with others who teach us the faith. Who is teaching the faith to members of your family? Talk about these teachers. Thank God for the time and insight they share with you. Then write thank-you notes to each of your teachers.

13—St. Lucia

Lucia was a young girl from Sicily who was burned at the stake for her faith. In Sweden, she is remembered each year on December 13, St. Lucia Day. Lucia means "light." In some Swedish families, this day is observed by the oldest daughter serving breakfast for the family while wearing a crown of candles on her head.

This is a day for service to others and joyful hospitality. Perhaps on this day the children of the household could prepare breakfast and serve their parents.

17—Dorothy Sayers (1893–1957)

Sayers was an English author of many books, including mystery novels, that reflected her Christian faith. One of her most famous is *The Man Born to Be King: A Play-Cycle on the Life of Our Lord and Savior Jesus Christ.*

This is a book adults in the family might enjoy. They could borrow it from the library and share the story with other family members.

January ✠

1—Holy Name of Jesus

Eight days following his birth, Jesus' parents—in obedience to the Law of Moses—took Jesus to be circumcised and "officially" gave him the name Jesus, which the Gospel tells us means "God saves." (See Matthew 1:18-21; Luke 1:31; 2:21.)

Look up and then talk about the meaning of each family member's name. Why was each person given the name? How appropriate is it to the person who bears it? Thank God for your names.

18—The Confession of St. Peter

This day remembers the witness of Peter who first recognized and bore witness to Jesus as God's promised savior (Matthew 16:16; Mark 8:29; Luke 9:20). Each of us is challenged by Jesus' question to Peter: "Who do you say that I am?"

This day invites us to explore our understanding of Jesus as the Christ. Have a discussion about the ways, in word and deed,

each of us can affirm that Jesus is our promised savior.

25—The Conversion of St. Paul

Acts 9:1-20 recounts the conversion of Saul, later referred to as Paul. The story of how this persecutor of the church was transformed into a great missionary is a witness to God's power in human life. On this day we pause to consider God's power to change lives and examine ways that God is changing lives today.

The story from Acts is well suited to a mini-play. Read it together several times so different members can take the parts of Saul, Ananias, and the voice of the risen Christ. Let each person start a faith-story diary and write a paragraph or draw a picture in it today. Ask yourselves, How do I see God alive in my family today?

February ✠

2—The Presentation of Jesus

Forty days after Jesus' birth, Mary and Joseph took him to be dedicated to God at the temple in Jerusalem. During the visit, they encountered an old man named

Simeon, who was promised that he would not die until he saw God's savior. Read that story in Luke 2:22-40.

This day is also Groundhog Day. Though the two celebrations may seem unrelated, the secular festival has its roots in the religious significance of this day. Research the library or Internet to discover this interesting connection.

14—St. Valentine (269)

Valentine was a bishop of Terni, Italy, who suffered martyrdom for his Christian faith. As one of the church's saints, Valentine was venerated by the early church. In the early fifteenth-century poetry of Chaucer, Valentine began to be associated with springtime love. The centuries that followed served to enlarge this connection.

Look at the ideas suggested for this day under the final section, "Special Days in the Civic Calendar." As part of the customs usually associated with this day, it would be fun to hold a Bible "scavenger hunt" in which family members see how many of the verses they can find that contain the word *love*. Read some of these together; let each person choose a favorite and explain why they like it.

18—Martin Luther (1483–1546)

The great reformer Martin Luther ushered in the Protestant Reformation. He is the spiritual leader of the Protestant denomination that bears his name. Luther's courage and faith, though sorely tested, remains an inspiration for all Christians.

If you can get a copy, sing or read together Luther's most popular hymn, "A Mighty Fortress Is Our God." This is often referred to as the battle hymn of the Reformation. Discuss what each person thinks the hymn means. What image do you have of a "fortress," and in what circumstances do you need God as a strong defense?

March ✠

10—Harriet Tubman (died 1913)

Harriet Tubman was born a slave in 1821 in the state of Maryland. When her master's estate was to be sold following his death, she fled to freedom in Pennsylvania. After tasting freedom for herself, she wanted others to experience this gift. She worked at many part-time jobs until she had enough money to undertake her first rescue effort, helping free her sister and two nieces. Over her lifetime, Harriet rescued more than 300 people. Eventually her network of homes and churches that helped slaves escape became known as the Underground Railroad. Harriet was often compared to Moses, who led the Hebrews out of Egypt.

Harriet Tubman's courage and thirst for justice are wonderful examples for us today. Which peoples of the world still do not enjoy freedom? With your family, be alert to newspaper features and television documentaries that expose the continued existence of slavery—especially the slavery of children. Ask your pastor what the church is doing to speak out against such abuse of human rights. Talk about the many privileges our freedom gives us, thank God for that freedom, and pray for those many people who are not free.

17—St. Patrick of Ireland (389–461)

When he was a young boy, Patrick was stolen from his home in England and enslaved by Irish raiders. After a number of years, he escaped and returned to his home; but later, Patrick returned as a missionary to his former captors in Ireland. Although this day has largely become a secular holiday, families might include in their worship

this prayer of St. Patrick (perhaps as a mealtime blessing over Irish stew):

> *May the strength of God pilot us.*
> *May the power of God preserve us.*
> *May the wisdom of God instruct us.*
> *May the hand of God protect us.*
> *May the way of God direct us.*
> *May the shield of God defend us.*
> *May the host of God guard us*
> *against the snares of evil*
> *and the temptations of the world.*
> *May Christ be with us,*
> *Christ before us,*
> *Christ in us,*
> *Christ over us.*
> *May your salvation, O Lord,*
> *be always ours this day*
> *and forevermore.*

Shamrocks are a popular symbol for this day. St. Patrick is said to have used a shamrock to teach Irish people about the Triune God. Make shamrock decorations from green construction paper and play Celtic music, if possible.

25—The Annunciation to Mary

Nine months before Christmas Day, this date remembers God's announcement to Mary through the angel Gabriel that she would bear the Son of God. Luke 1:26-38 narrates this encounter and contains the Song of Mary ("Magnificat") in which Mary sings of God's salvation for the poor and oppressed. This is a day to read or sing Mary's Song or to play a recording of the "Magnificat" by one of the world's outstanding composers. Some church traditions accord the color blue to days that remember Mary's devotion to God. Perhaps you might use blue napkins at your dinner table or wear a blue article of clothing.

April ✠

4—Martin Luther King Jr. (1929–1968)

Though our civic calendar remembers this leader on his birthday—a Monday in January—Christians honor Martin Luther King Jr. on this day, when he was murdered. King was a leader of the civil rights movement and a champion of nonviolence. His witness calls all of us to work for reconciliation.

On this day, pray for racial equality, harmony, and justice. Consider ways your family can work to overcome prejudice that divides neighbors near and far. Have an older child look up and read to the family a portion of King's famous "I Have a Dream" speech. Talk about this dream as it relates to God's promise of a new kingdom.

9—Dietrich Bonhoeffer (1906–1945)

Bonhoeffer was executed for his opposition to Hitler during World War II. One of his books, *The Cost of Discipleship*, speaks of the radical call to obedience that comes when we follow Jesus. The book is one of the classics in Christian literature.

Look up information about Dietrich Bonhoeffer in an encyclopedia or on the Internet and present this to your family. Then talk about commitment to God as your number-one loyalty. Is it possible today for other commitments to supersede this loyalty to God? Has this happened to any of you?

May ✠

8—Julian of Norwich (1342–1425)

A member of a monastic order and a Christian mystic, Julian is best known for her spiritual writings *(Revelations of Divine Love)*, which express deep devotion to Christ. Julian's profound insights about faith have influenced much devotional literature.

One important devotional practice is keeping silence. Experiment with silent mediation by eating a portion of your dinner meal in silence, or sit in silent prayer or meditation for five minutes at the end of the meal. Then invite everyone to reflect on their experience. How did the silence awaken you to each other and to God?

27—John Calvin (1509–1564)

A father of Presbyterianism and a major theologian of the reformed tradition, Calvin's writings emphasize God's grace and the gratitude that ought to be our response to that grace. Calvin also believed strongly in ecumenism. In a time when Christians were deeply divided, Calvin struggled for the unity of the church.

Offer a prayer of thanks for the evidence we see of God's grace in Christians of all traditions.

31—The Visitation of Mary to Elizabeth

This day commemorates pregnant Mary's visit to her cousin Elizabeth, who also was pregnant with a child foretold by the prophets. Read about this visit and about the subsequent birth of Elizabeth's son, John, in Luke 1:39-80.

Do you know a family who is expecting a child? Send them a card to express your congratulations and joy. Remember with gratitude how children are gifts of God who bring with them the promise that God will not abandon the world.

June

14—Basil the Great (329–379)

A pastor, theologian, and archbishop of the early church, St. Basil struggled to rid the church of false teaching. He was also a champion for the needs of the sick and poor people in his land.

Think of sick people in your church, family, or neighborhood who need your prayers. As a family, pray for those people. Then plan a visit or a phone call to cheer them up, or work together to make a card and letter to send them.

22—Thomas More (1478–1535)

This English politician, writer, and scholar refused to compromise his godly conscience when he was pressured by King Henry VIII to support a break with the church at Rome over Henry's desire to divorce his wife. Because he was true to his convictions, More was imprisoned and eventually beheaded.

The temptation and pressure to compromise our principles and morals can be great. From what areas of society and life do you feel pressure to compromise? With your family, pray for courage and strength to be true to your God-given convictions.

24—The Birth of John the Baptist

John was the divinely promised son of Zechariah and Elizabeth. He has been called the greatest prophet to prepare the way for Jesus' ministry. John lived his life pointing to Jesus as God's gift to the world and preparing his people to receive Jesus as their savior.

Read the story of John's birth in Luke 1:57-80. Talk together about John's example: What does it mean to live our lives pointing to Jesus?

July ✠

11—St. Benedict of Nursia (480–547)

Founder of the Benedictine monastic order, St. Benedict developed a "rule," or set of guidelines, designed to instill in his monks the values of prayer, work, and hospitality to strangers. The Rule of Benedict is still followed by Benedictines.

How might we live our lives so as to be more open to people we do not know? In all your dealings today, make an extra effort to show kindness to others and to look into the eyes of strangers with whom you speak. Listen with care to everyone you talk with; then reflect on what a difference such attentiveness can make.

24—Thomas á Kempis (1380–1471)

Thomas á Kempis was a German monk who preached about Christ, copied manuscripts, and wrote books. He is best remembered for his devotional classic *The Imitation of Christ,* a book that expresses deep love and commitment to Jesus Christ.

Copies of *The Imitation of Christ* are available in paperback and would make a fine addition to any home library. In the book, Thomas á Kempis asks his readers, "What can the world offer you, without Jesus?" Such a question leads us to clarify what we value most in our lives—and this would make a good topic for dinner conversation this day.

28—Johann Sebastian Bach (1685–1750)

A composer, organist, and church music director, Bach has had enormous influence on sacred music. His *St. Matthew's Passion* and *St. John's Passion* are marvelous musical expressions of these Gospel stories and traditions.

Listen to selections of Bach's music today, either from a recording you own or on public radio broadcasts.

August ✠

6—Victims of the Atomic Bombings (1945)

On this day in 1945, the United States dropped an atomic bomb on Hiroshima, Japan. Three days later, a similar bomb was dropped on Nagasaki, Japan. At that time, we were at war with Japan; and we justified the bombings by saying they would end the war more quickly. However, these bomb blasts wreaked unspeakable horror, pain, and mass destruction. They also opened the world to the terrifying prospect of nuclear warfare. Such a danger exists as long as the weapons and technology are available.

This is a day to pray for the victims of the bombing, for peace and tolerance, and for a worldwide ban on all weapons of mass destruction.

13—Florence Nightingale (1820–1910)

Florence Nightingale was the founder of modern nursing. She dedicated her life to caring for sick people and for those injured in war. Nightingale placed the comfort and needs of others before her own. Such compassion befits all who follow the way of Jesus.

To whom might we show compassion on this day? How can we remind ourselves that by showing kindness to other people, we are showing kindness to Jesus himself? Encourage everyone in the family to show compassion to one another as a way to begin showing kindness to others.

28—Augustine of Hippo (354–430)

St. Augustine was a theologian, teacher, and bishop of the early church. He is one of the most important and influential of all Western Christians. Augustine's personal faith story, *Confessions,* reveals his deep desire to discover and then do what is right. This desire shaped his life as a dedicated Christian.

As your evening prayer, use the following words of Augustine—one of the many beautiful prayers attributed to the saint:

> *Watch, O Lord, with those who*
> *wake or watch or weep tonight,*
> *and give your angels and saints*
> *charge over those who sleep.*
> *Tend your sick ones, O Lord Christ,*
> *Rest your weary ones,*
> *Bless your dying ones,*
> *Soothe your suffering ones,*
> *Pity your afflicted ones,*
> *Shield your joyous ones,*
> *And all for your love's sake.*

31—John Bunyan (1627–1688)

An English author and Baptist lay preacher, Bunyan wrote the Christian classic *Pilgrim's Progress,* an allegory of a Christian's journey through this life.

Several illustrated editions of this book are available. Consider purchasing a copy and reading it aloud over successive nights. Allow time to talk about what you read. The imagery in the book will spark anyone's imagination.

September ✠

5—Mother Teresa (1910–1997)

Teresa was a humble woman from Albania who dedicated her life to serving others. Sometime after becoming a nun, she started an order called Missionaries of Charity in order to care for sick and dying people in Calcutta, India. Her unconditional compassion inspired millions of people. She believed that in loving the unwanted and unloved, she was truly loving Jesus. For her work she was awarded the Nobel Peace Prize.

How can we learn to think of others as "Jesus in disguise"? What difference might such a way of thinking make in how we treat others? Today, show kindness to someone who is sick or in the hospital. Make a family greeting card together; then, if possible, pay a brief visit to deliver your card and good wishes.

13—John Chrysostom (347–407)

Pastor and theologian, St. John was called Chrysostom—"golden-tongued"—for his eloquence in preaching. Chrysostom criticized the indifference of the wealthy and powerful people and proclaimed the need to live the message of love found in the Gospel.

Give thanks to God for the person who preaches the Gospel in your church. Take time today to send your pastor a note of encouragement. Put a stick of gum or a small mint in the envelope to make your note special.

18—Louis Pasteur (1822–1895)

Pasteur was a devout Roman Catholic who dedicated himself to the struggle against disease. His work contributed greatly to medical research.

How does our faith enable each of us to work for the welfare of all persons? Who are the persons who work to take care of us? You might take a moment to send an appreciation card to your family doctor, thanking her or him for being so dedicated to helping those who are ill. Mention that you thought of this because today is Louis Pasteur Day.

October

4—Francis of Assisi (1181–1226)

Dedicated to a life of simplicity, Francis reached out to the poor and the sick. He is remembered for his love of all God's creation. Tradition also credits him with the custom of setting up a crèche at Christmas. Francis is said to have authored a beautiful prayer that would serve well at family mealtime worship.

> *Lord, make me an instrument*
> *of your peace.*
> *Where there is hatred,*
> *let me sow love;*
> *where there is injury, pardon;*
> *where there is doubt, faith;*
> *where there is despair, hope;*
> *where there is darkness, light;*
> *where there is sadness, joy.*
> *O Divine Master, grant*
> *that I may not seek so much*

to be consoled as to console,
to be understood as to understand,
to be loved as to love.
For it is in giving that we receive,
it is in pardoning
that we are pardoned,
and it is in dying that we are born
to eternal life.

Because of St. Francis's love for animals, some Christian traditions show special attention to pets on this day. If you have a pet, give him or her a little extra time and attention. Thank God for all the earth's creatures—and the privilege to enjoy one of them as a pet!

17—Ignatius of Antioch (died 107)

Tradition remembers Ignatius as a disciple of St. John the Apostle and one of the early martyrs to his faith. He is thought to have been fed to the lions in the Roman Coliseum by the Roman Emperor Trajan. Many Christians have died for their faith and commitment to Jesus Christ. Their lives and deaths are testimony to God's power and promise.

Ask your pastor where Christians today are suffering for their faith. Be sure to include these Christians in your family prayers today.

31—Reformation Day (1517)

On All Hallows Eve (later to become Halloween) of 1517, Martin Luther posted his ninety-five theses or arguments on the door of Wittenberg Chapel. The theses criticized what Luther considered false teachings in the church, and they touched off a movement of reform that has since become known as the Protestant Reformation.

On this day, we remember with humility that the church of Jesus Christ needs constant reforming as we strive to understand and fulfill God's purpose for us in this world.

Family Baptismal Birthdays

Baptism anniversaries are joyous occasions that should be celebrated by the entire family. Because of parents' attention to birthdays, children come to regard these anniversaries as significant. Likewise, our attention as Christian parents to baptism anniversaries will help our children value the anniversaries of their "birth" into the community of Christ. When we celebrate each family member's baptismal birthday, we help shape a sense of Christian identity and shared communion in Christ.

If necessary, do some research into the dates for each baptism; then mark the dates in red on the family calendar. While you're researching, see what else you can unearth: baptismal gowns, church bulletins, baptismal certificates, photographs, greeting cards, and gifts. Why not let the entire family assemble these items into special memory books?

Here are a few suggestions for ways to celebrate baptismal birthdays:

Cross of Honor

In our family, the one who celebrates a baptismal birthday is honored by wearing a special cross around the neck throughout mealtime celebrations. Since we have several such crosses, the birthday person can choose which one to wear.

Candle Lighting

For the mealtime prayer, consider using a special candle reserved just for baptismal birthdays. Let the "birthday" person have the honor of lighting the candle and offering a special mealtime prayer.

Special Liturgy

Once the meal is ended, consider using a special liturgy that celebrates baptismal remembrance. Here are elements that might be included in such a home liturgy:

Scripture Reading

The liturgy could include the text from Romans 6:3-4:

> *Do you not know*
> *that all of us who have been*
> *baptized into Christ Jesus*
> *were baptized into his death?*
> *Therefore we have been buried*
> *with him by baptism into death,*
> *so that, just as Christ was raised*
> *from the dead by the glory*
> *of the Father,*
> *so we too might walk in newness*
> *of life.*

Hymn

Singing is an integral part of any celebration. Check your hymnal for a favorite baptismal hymn. By singing a verse or two of the hymn, you can help connect the family celebration with memories of the baptismal celebration in church.

Signing of the Cross

The sign of the cross recalls the new identity of Christians that we receive as a gift in baptism. In our home, we place a small bowl of water on the table. All of us, one by

one, wet our thumbs and make the sign of the cross on the forehead of the person to our left. As we do this, we speak the name of the person and say, "*(name)*, remember your baptism and be thankful. You are a disciple of Jesus Christ."

Even though we have repeated this ceremony many times and for many years, it still brings a moment of reverent silence because we are aware that something holy is taking place.

Apostles' Creed

Families might choose to repeat together this earliest of Christian creeds, which offers a joint statement of our baptismal faith. Its origins reach back to baptism in the early church.

Prayer of Thanksgiving

Introduce the prayer with "The Lord be with you." The rest of the family responds with the words in bold:

> *The Lord be with you.*
> **And also with you.**
> *Let us give thanks to the Lord our God.*
> **It is right to give God thanks and praise.**

This prayer is best prayed in unison:

> *God of water and oil,*
> *you are the giver of new life.*
> *We thank you for making us your children through baptism.*
> *Today we remember and rejoice in _____'s baptism.*
> *Continue to work your grace in _____'s life,*
> *and help us all to be faithful disciples of Jesus our Lord.*

Lord's Prayer

Conclude with the prayer Jesus taught his disciples.

Blessing

This honor could be given to the person whose baptism occasioned the celebration. The family could stand and join hands, or one person could raise his or her hands over the other family members as this blessing is spoken:

> *May we continue to grow in the grace and knowledge of Jesus Christ, our Lord and Savior.*
> **Amen.**
> *Bless the Lord.*
> **The Lord's name be praised.**

A Small Gift

Some families may want to give the birthday person a gift chosen to nurture faith: a small cross to wear around the neck or one to hang in the bedroom; a CD of Christian music; a Bible coloring book; a Christian videotape; a book of Bible stories; a collection of prayers. It is not necessary to spend a great deal of money. Gift giving brings a further element of festivity, and it can help to focus on the spiritual significance of this event.

Special Dessert

Families may wish to conclude their celebration by sharing a favorite dessert of the birthday person. For young children, cake and celebrations are strongly connected, but any special dessert can add an extra touch to the celebration.

Special Days in the Civic Calendar

We who belong to Jesus Christ live with multiple calendars. Because we are citizens of our country, we also celebrate the holidays that form our culture's festive life. Unfortunately, many times these holidays are tainted by commercial interests that equate celebrating with shopping and spending money. The ideas below suggest that we shape our celebrations of cultural holidays in ways consistent with our faith and values. One way to do this is by drawing each holiday into the ritual of family mealtime or bedtime prayer. For this purpose, prayers are included as part of the suggestions for each holiday.

February ✠

Presidents' Day (Third Monday)

After the United States government abandoned separate observances for Washington's and Lincoln's birthdays and moved the holiday to a Monday, our culture has paid less and less attention to the significance of these leaders. Families might work to reclaim a focus of honoring leaders who made significant contributions to their country. Good biographies have been written about both of these early leaders; check with a local library for ones appropriate to your family. You might want to read sections of these after a festive meal or at bedtime.

Creator of all peoples,
Ruler of the nations,
you hold justice and mercy
in your hands.
We thank you for leaders
who have struggled against the evils
of their time
and worked for your purposes.
Give us the courage to overcome evil
with good
and to follow where you lead.
With grateful hearts
we share this meal.

Valentine's Day (February 14)

Until the late fourteenth century, St. Valentine, who suffered martyrdom on February 14, was remembered as just another of the church's many saints. In the early 1400s, however, Valentine began to be associated with romantic love and courtship; and eventually he became the patron of lovers.

Today, Valentine's Day is celebrated with the exchange of cards and candy among schoolmates, friends, and family. Society appears to have little interest in remembering St. Valentine himself, preferring to maintain an emphasis on romantic love.

Families might choose to remember St. Valentine (check your library or the Internet for fascinating biographies and legends), or they may prefer to deepen the understanding of love to that of "servant love" by planning acts of self-giving love for one another.

God of love,
we are created by you for love.
Thank you for families and friends
with whom we share affection.
Keep us always in the center
of your love,
which thinks of others
before ourselves.
Make this day one of joyful
celebration and laughter
for the blessings you bring us
in one another.
Through Jesus Christ our Lord.

May ✠

Mother's Day (Second Sunday)

Seeking to honor her own mother and all mothers, Anna Jarvis persuaded her mother's church to hold a special service. The first such observation was held in 1908 on the second Sunday in May—the anniversary of her mother's death. In 1914, Congress proclaimed the second Sunday in May as Mother's Day.

Instead of taking Mom out for dinner this year, why not let the rest of the family create a homemade extravaganza featuring some of Mom's favorite foods? For example, the children, with someone's help (not Mom's), could plan and prepare a backyard barbecue, a picnic by a lake, or even the best pizza in town, served with candlelight, fine china, and cloth napkins.

Cards or gifts can be homemade, too. And instead of visiting a florist, make your own bouquets and table arrangements by buying a few carnations and adding greenery from around the backyard. Strive for maximum participation and creativity, so that everyone is able to lend their talents to the event.

Because Mother's Day often coincides with Good Shepherd Sunday—the Fourth Sunday of Easter—the prayer given for this day (on page 55) could be used.

Memorial Day (Last Monday)

Memorial Day commemorates those who have died in defense of our country. It originated in 1868 as a time to remember the dead of the Civil War and to pray for national reconciliation. As the holiday evolved, it came to honor all United States citizens who died in war. This is a day to mourn the horrors of war—the sorrow, death, and destruction that come as its natural results. It is also traditional for families to decorate the graves of those who died, hence the older name for the holiday, "Decoration Day."

Families gather on this long weekend for picnics and other outside activities because it also signals the approach of summer and summer vacation.

Memorial Day invites families to remember their own histories and how previous generations have served their fellow humans with sacrifice and courage. It is a good time to open photograph albums, reminisce about the past, and share the family story.

God of the generations,
we bless you for all
who have unselfishly given
themselves in service to others,
especially when that sacrifice cost
them their lives.
Hasten the day when we shall make
war no more
and live together in peace.
Strengthen this family
so that we will always defend the
rights of the poor and oppressed.
Gladden this day of feasting and fun
with gratitude for the life
you have given us.
Through Jesus Christ our Lord.

June ✠

Father's Day (Third Sunday)

This holiday began in 1909 when Sonora Louise Smart Dodd organized a church service in memory of her father, Civil War veteran William Smart. Father's Day proved a natural inclusion to a civil calendar that had recently added Mother's Day. Not until 1966, however, did the day become an official national holiday. The suggested activities for Mother's Day would work well for Father's Day, too.

Identify Dad's favorite food, choose an activity that all enjoy, and then build a celebration day around this core.

God of all families,
we thank you for the gift
of parents and children.
As a mother hen tends her young,
as the father welcomes the prodigal
home,
so you parent us all with a heart of
selfless giving.
Bind us in the love that you freely
give to all
so that we will have more than
enough to share with neighbors and
strangers alike.
Bless fathers and mothers
and the children of all households
with grace and joy.
Through Jesus Christ our Lord.

July ✠

Independence Day (July 4)

This day recalls the signing of the Declaration of Independence from Britain in 1776 and celebrates political freedom in which a majority can choose its own leaders. Always a festive day for U.S. communities, this day is filled with picnics, games, parades, and fireworks.

Most families may already have long-standing traditions by which they observe this day. One thing to emphasize in all the celebrations, however, is that the gift of freedom carries responsibility. Consider making this day a focus on freedom *for* responsibility rather than freedom *from* responsibility: in your plans and preparations, delegate important jobs for every family member to complete in order to have a successful celebration.

> *Lord of the nations,*
> *to whom we all owe trust*
> *and obedience,*
> *thank you for the land*
> *which is our home*
> *and the people with whom we live.*
> *Forge the diversity*
> *which is our country*
> *into a unity of shared respect*
> *and neighborliness.*
> *Heal our wounds,*
> *purge our sins,*
> *and mend our flaws,*
> *so that we might be a blessing*
> *to the world.*
> *Give us the pleasure of food*

> *and play this day*
> *as we join together in festivity.*
> *And make our hearts grateful*
> *for the privilege of our liberty*
> *with which we are free to serve you.*
> *Through Jesus Christ our Lord.*

September ✠

Labor Day Weekend (First Monday)

This holiday traces its origins back to the late 1800s, when labor leaders called attention to poor working conditions and the need for fair compensation. Following the Industrial Revolution, these issues were of critical importance. Labor Day honors all the laborers in our land; and it both remembers and calls attention to the importance of economic justice in the workplace.

In addition, this long weekend signals the end of summer and the beginning of a new school year. It is a chance for families to have one final time of rest and recreation. Many families plan reunions and picnics over this weekend. One good way to honor the day is by undertaking a project around the home in which all can participate.

When they work together for a common goal, families can have fun and celebrate the creativity of shared labor.

God of all power and love,
with whom we have nothing to fear,
thank you for Christ's victory
over the forces of evil.
With joy and playfulness
we ridicule evil.
remembering how you freed us
to live in trust.
Keep our neighborhoods safe this
night with mutual concern
and watchfulness.
Give cheer to children
and parents alike
as we delight in sweet celebration.
Through Jesus Christ our Lord.

October ✠

Halloween (October 31)

November 1, All Saints' Day, sometimes bears the name All Hallows Day. Thus, the night before November 1 received the name All Hallows Eve—which later was shortened to Halloween. Many aspects of Halloween have roots among the peoples of northern Europe, who gathered at the start of their winter season (which began on November 1) to light bonfires and welcome souls of the dead, who returned home on this night for warmth and hospitality.

From this primitive observance rose the practice of costuming—either to welcome the expected visitors or else to hide from them. Trick-or-treat customs today reflect these origins and invite families and neighbors to share in playful hospitality.

Many families have begun to practice safe and more responsible ways to participate in this festival. Many Christian families tie their celebrations to the church festival, All Saints' Day—a time to honor and give thanks for faithful followers of Jesus who have died.

This festival would be a good time for families to name fears and submit them to Christ, before whom all darkness is as light.

God of all power and love,
with whom we have nothing to fear,
thank you for Christ's victory over
the forces of evil.
With joy and playfulness
we ridicule evil,
remembering how you freed us
to live in trust.

*Keep our neighborhoods safe
this night.
Give us all a spirit of mutual
concern and watchfulness.
Give cheer to children and
parents alike
as we delight in sweet celebration.
Through Jesus Christ our Lord.*

November ✠

Thanksgiving (Fourth Thursday)

In 1621, Pilgrims in the Massachusetts Bay colony celebrated a good harvest by sharing a three-day feast with the Native Americans who had helped them. This is the origin of our holiday of thanks. In 1789, President George Washington proclaimed an official day of thanksgiving for the new country. However, a fixed date was not set until 1863, when Abraham Lincoln designated the fourth Thursday in November as Thanksgiving Day.

For many Christians, Thanksgiving recalls the New Testament story in which Jesus healed ten men of leprosy, and only one of them returned to thank him (Luke 17: 11-19). This is a day for families to gather for prayer, thanksgiving, good conversation, and good food. It is also a time to share in the tasks of setting the table, preparing the food, and washing up. No one should be left to do these tasks alone. For many families, this day also involves sharing with others. If you have no one with whom to share this day, consider inviting others who would otherwise eat alone. Before or after eating, invite children and adults alike to describe one or two personal blessings for which they are thankful. Finally, be sure to tell one another how each of you is God's gift to the others.

*God of the autumn harvest,
your generosity is without bounds,
and your love knows no end.
We thank you for this bounty given
for our enjoyment
and for all gathered here
with whom it is shared.
Remember all for whom this day
will be another of unrelieved hunger.
Let your compassion overflow
in the hearts of all who prosper,
so that we will soon see the day
of your promised blessing,
when all will sit at your table
to feast in joy.
Through Jesus Christ our Redeemer.*